**KU-377-311**

# Dictionary of
# Scottish
# surnames

## A guide to Scottish surnames and clan names

**SCOTLAND***on*SUNDAY

HarperCollins Publishers,
Westerhill Road, Bishopbriggs, Glasgow G64 2QT
www.collins.co.uk

First published 1953
Revised edition 1989

This special edition produced for
Scotland on Sunday 2007

© Clan House of Edinburgh Ltd, 1953, 1989

ISBN 9780007801671

All rights reserved. No part of this publication may be
reproduced, stored in a retrieval system or transmitted, in
any form or by any means, electronic, mechanical,
photocopying, recording or otherwise, without the prior
permission of the publisher.

This book is sold subject to the conditions that it shall not,
by way of trade or otherwise, be lent, re-sold, hired out or
otherwise circulated without the publisher's prior consent in
any form of binding or cover other than that in which it is
published and without a similar condition including this
condition being imposed on the subsequent purchaser.

The publishers regret that they cannot enter into
correspondence regarding personal family histories. A list
of relevant books and organisations is given on p.96.

Printed in the UK by CPI Bookmarque, Croydon, CR0 4TD

# CONTENTS

# INTRODUCTION

An old Gaelic proverb says, 'Remember the men from whence you came.' By 'men', of course, it means humankind, embracing women, which in fact sums up how unfair — and distorting — is the basic principle of surnames. By law, throughout Britain, we are required to take the surname of our father and his father before him, not that of our mother or even her father's family. The word 'surname' refers to another name which has been 'added on' to a first or Christian name. Just how, and when, your family name was added to a forbear's first name can vary enormously. In Lowland Scotland some territorial names were being introduced as surnames in the 11th century, mostly by landed people. Then we see centuries of surname proliferation as men became known by their trades ('Taillour', 'Porter'), proximity to geographical features ('Wood', 'Burnbank'), personal characteristics or colouring ('Little', 'Reid'), or by connection to their father's name ('Johnson', 'Donaldson').

This last style, called patronymics, was popular when surnames came widely into use in the Highlands in the 16th century. Gradually (and not until this century in the Northern Isles), the patronymic system was replaced by the adoption of a fixed family name taken from an ancestral figure, or 'namefather', like Gregor, brother of King Kenneth MacAlpine in the 9th century, from whom the MacGregors take their name. This removed the practice of members of a generation taking their surnames from their own fathers' Christian names. John Robertson's father was *Robert* Williamson whose father was *William* Thomson whose father was *Thomas* Davidson whose father was David. . . . The process becomes confusing when you find that your MacDonald forbear was the son of a Donald Campbell.

In the great ancestry game, you will learn quickly that your surname is only the tip of the genetic iceberg. If your genuinely MacDonald forbear had found himself isolated in the heart of Campbell country ten generations ago, had married Jean Campbell and seen his sons and grandsons married to Campbell girls, you could find yourself today with a bank of forbears totalling 1,022, all of whom were Campbells except yourself and the nine named MacDonald in the direct male line. But the even more awesome thought is that if just *one* of those 1,022 forbears (your parents, four grandparents, eight great-grandparents, etc) had died in childhood, you would not be here today. So you are much, much more than just your surname.

This book is a key to understanding all the other names which you are heir to. A simple, easy-to-use key if you remember the following rules:

★ The sound of a name is generally more important than its spelling, which would have been standardised only comparatively recently. Shakespeare, who was somewhat literate, spelt his own surname in over twenty different ways in his lifetime.

★ Including spelling variations, there are over 16,000 Scottish surnames, but fewer than 3,000 of these are of Highland origin and associated with clans. The majority of Scots throughout history lived in the Lowlands and developed a culture which produced the majority of Scotland's genius but without the glamour which is now associated with their Highland cousins.

★ *Mac* is part of many Scottish surnames and simply means 'son'. It is popularly believed that names beginning with *Mc* are of Irish origin and those with *Mac*, Scottish. This is not the case. *Mac* is the standardised prefix used today, but a hundred years ago it was commonly abbreviated in written records to *Mc* or even *M'*.

★ The association of certain common names with a clan, e.g. Reid, Smith, is generally because there were prominent families of that name connected with that clan and not that it had the monopoly of ruddy-faced or red-haired people or of clansmen with metal-working skills.

Micheil MacDonald, FSA Scot.
Director, Highland Tryst Museum
Crieff

# WHAT IS YOUR CLAN OR DISTRICT CONNECTION?

Scottish surnames alphabetically arranged to show clan or sept connection, or approximate district or century earliest known in Scotland.

Cross-references to other names in this list are printed in capitals. The names of associated clans (whose histories are given in *Clans of Scotland* starting on page 53) are printed in italic type.

| SURNAME | CLAN OR DISTRICT SOURCE |
|---|---|
| ABBOT, ABBOTT | Fife etc. 14th c.; *MACNAB* |
| ABBOTSON | *MACNAB* |
| ABERCROMBIE | Fife (place, now St Monans) 15th c. |
| ABERNETHY | Strathearn 12th c.; *FRASER*; *LESLIE* |
| ADAIR | Galloway 14th c.; from EDGAR |
| ADAM, ADAMS | Fife etc. 13th c.; *GORDON* |
| ADAMSON | Berwickshire 13th c., Aberdeen 14th c.; *GORDON*; *MACKINTOSH* |
| ADDIE, ADIE | Fife 13th c.; *GORDON* |
| ADDISON | Peeblesshire etc. 14th c.; *GORDON* |
| AFFLECK | From AUCHINLECK, Angus 14th c. |
| AGNEW | Galloway 11th c. |
| AIKMAN | Lanarkshire 13th c. |
| AINSLIE | Roxburghshire etc. 13th c. |
| AIRD | Ayrshire 16th c. |
| AIRLIE | *OGILVIE* |
| AIRTH | Stirlingshire 12th c.; *GRAHAM* |
| AITCHISON | E. Lothian 14th c.; *GORDON* |
| AITKEN, AIKEN | Aberdeen 15th c.; *GORDON* |
| AITKENHEAD | Lanarkshire (place) 13th c. |
| ALASTAIR | Same as ALEXANDER |
| ALCOCK | From ALLAN |
| ALEXANDER | *MACALISTER*; *MACDONALD* MACDONNELL of Glengarry |
| ALISON, ALLISON | From MACALISTER: also ALLANSON |
| ALLAN, ALLEN | Same as MACALLAN |
| ALLANACH | Aberdeenshire, see MACALLAN |
| ALLANSON | From MACALLAN |
| ALLARDYCE | Mearns (place) 13th c.; *GRAHAM* |
| ALLISTER | Same as ALEXANDER |
| ALPIN, ALPINE | Clan ALPIN |
| ALVES | Moray (Alves) 13th c. |
| AMBROSE | Glasgow 15th c., Edinburgh etc. 17th c. |
| ANDERSON | Peebles etc. 13th c. *ROSS* Islay, *MACDONALD* |
| ANDISON | From ANDERSON |
| ANDREW, ANDREWS | Dumfries, Aberdeen 14th c.; *ROSS* |
| ANGUS | Angus county 13th c.; *MACINNES* |
| ANNAL, ANNALL | Fife 16th c. |
| ANNAN, ANNAND | Annandale, also Angus 13th c. |
| ANSTRUTHER | Fife (place) 13th c. |

| SURNAME | CLAN OR DISTRICT SOURCE |
| --- | --- |
| ANTHONY | Roxburghshire 13th c. |
| ARBUCKLE | Lanarkshire (place) 15th c. |
| ARBUTHNOT | Kincardineshire (place) 12th c. |
| ARCHER | Ayrshire 13th c., Angus 15th c. |
| ARCHIBALD | Roxburghshire 14th c.; also GILLESPIE |
| ARGYL | *MACGREGOR* |
| ARMOUR | 'Armourer': Peebles, Angus etc. 14th c. |
| ARMSTRONG | Clan *ARMSTRONG* |
| ARNOLD, ARNOULD | Selkirkshire, W. Lothian, 13th c. |
| ARNOT, ARNOTT | Kinross-shire 12th c., Ayrshire 15th c. |
| ARROL | Perthshire (Errol) 16th c.; *HAY* |
| ARROWSMITH | *MACGREGOR* |
| ARTHUR, ARTHURSON | *MACARTHUR* |
| ASKEY | *MACLEOD* of Lewis |
| ATKIN, ATKINS | Same as AITKEN |
| ATKINSON | Same as AITCHISON |
| AUCHINCLOSS | Ayrshire (Kilmarnock) 15th c. |
| AUCHINLECK | Ayrshire (Cumnock) 13th c. |
| AUCHTERLONIE | Angus (place near Forfar) 13th c. |
| AULAY | *MACAULAY*; *MACLEOD* of Lewis |
| AULD | Ayrshire and Perth 13th c. |
| AUSTIN | *KEITH* |
| AYSON | *MACINTOSH* of Glentilt |
| AYTON, AYTOUN | Berwickshire (place) 12th c.; *HOME* |
| BADENOCH | Badenoch to Aberdeenshire 15th c. |
| BAIKIE | Orkney 16th c. |
| BAILEY, BAILLIE | Lothian 14th c., Lamington 16th c. |
| BAIN | Perth 14th c.; *MACKAY* |
| BAINES | Fife (St Andrews) 16th c. |
| BAIRD | Lanarkshire 13th c. |
| BAIRNSFATHER | East Lothian 16th c. |
| BAIRNSON | Caithness 16th c.; *MATHESON* |
| BALCANQUALL | Fife (Strathmiglo) 14th c. |
| BALD | Peeblesshire and Perth 13th c. |
| BALDERSTON | W. Lothian (place) 13th c. |
| BALFOUR | Fife (Markinch) 14th c. |
| BALLANTYNE | Hawick 15th c.; and from BANNATYNE |
| BALLINGALL | Kinross-shire (place) 15th c. |
| BALLOCH, BALLACH | Lennox 15th c., *MACDONALD* |
| BALMAIN | Kincardineshire (place) 16th c. |
| BALNEAVES | Angus 14th c.; *MURRAY* |
| BALSILLIE | Fife (Leslie) 16th c. |
| BANKS | Berwick 13th c.; Orkney 17th c. |
| BANNATYNE | *CAMPBELL*; *STUART* of Bute |
| BANNERMAN | Aberdeen 14th c.; *FORBES* |
| BAPTIE | Berwickshire 13th c. |
| BARBER, BARBOUR | Ayrshire 13th c. |
| BARCLAY | Aberdeenshire etc. 12th c. |
| BARD, BARDE | Same as BAIRD |
| BARKER | Stirlingshire and Lothians 13th c. |
| BARLAS | Perthshire 17th c. |
| BARNES, BARNS | Aberdeenshire 15th c. |
| BARNETSON | Caithness 16th c. |
| BARON, BARRON | Angus 15th c.; Inverness, *ROSE* |
| BARR | Ayrshire 14th c. |

| SURNAME | CLAN OR DISTRICT SOURCE |
|---|---|
| BARRACK | Aberdeenshire (Meldrum) 16th c. |
| BARRIE, BARRY | Angus 14th c.; *FARQUHARSON*; *GORDON* |
| BARROWDALE | *MACGREGOR* |
| BARTHOLOMEW | Midlothian 13th c.; *MACFARLANE* |
| BARTIE, BARTY, BARTLEMAN, BARTLET, BARLETT | From BARTHOLOMEW |
| BARTON | Ayrshire, Berwickshire 13th c. |
| BATCHELOR | E. Lothian 13th c., Angus 15th c. |
| BATHGATE | W. Lothian 13th c. |
| BAUCHOPE, BACHOP | From WAUCHOPE |
| BAXTER | Lothian 12th c.; *MACMILLAN* |
| BAYNE, BAYNES | See BAIN and BAINES |
| BEAN | *MACBEAN* |
| BEATH | *MACDONALD*; *MACLEAN* |
| BEATON | *MACLEAN*, and from BETHUNE |
| BEATSON | Dumfriesshire 14th c., Fife 17th c. |
| BEATTIE, BEATTY | Dumfriesshire etc. 14th c.; *MACBETH* |
| BEAUMONT | E. Fife 13th c. |
| BECK | Dumfriesshire 14th c. |
| BEE | Angus 16th c., Edinburgh etc. 17th c. |
| BEGBIE | Haddington 16th c. |
| BEGG | Lennox 13th c.; *DRUMMOND* |
| BEGLAND | *MACGREGOR* |
| BELFORD | Berwick 12th c., Stirling 14th c. |
| BELFRAGE | W. Fife, Kinross from BEVERIDGE |
| BELL | Dunkeld, Dumfries 13th c; *MACMILLAN* |
| BELTON | E. Lothian 13th c.; *MACBETH* |
| BENHAM | Kincardineshire (Benholm) 13th c. |
| BENNET, BENNETT | Roxburghshire 16th c., Fife 17th c. |
| BENNIE, BENNY | Gowrie 13th c., Aberdeen 14th c. |
| BENVIE | Dundee 13th c. |
| BENZIE, BENZIES | Aberdeenshire (Inverurie) 15th c. |
| BERNARD | Perthshire 13th c. |
| BERRIE, BERRY | Fife, Angus 14th c.; *FORBES* |
| BERTRAM | W. Fife 13th c., Edinburgh 15th c. |
| BERWICK | Berwick, to Roxburgh etc. 13th c. |
| BEST | Edinburgh 15th c., Aberdeen 17th c. |
| BETHUNE | Angus 12th c., Fife 13th c.; *MACBETH* *MACDONALD*; *MACLEOD* |
| BETT | Edinburgh 14th c., Fife, Angus 15th c. |
| BEVERIDGE | Fife 14th c. |
| BEWS, BEWES | Orkney 17th c. |
| BEY | From MACBEY; *MACLEAN* |
| BIE | Same as BEE |
| BIGAM, BIGGAM | Edinburgh 15th c. |
| BIGGAR | Lanarkshire 12th c. |
| BILSLAND | Ayrshire 16th c. |
| BINNIE | *MACBEAN* |
| BINNIE, BINNING | W. Lothian 13th c. |
| BIRD | Aberdeen 15th c., Edinburgh 16th c. |
| BIRNIE, BIRNEY | Elgin 13th c. and from MACBIRNIE |
| BIRRELL, BIRREL | Berwick 15th c., Glasgow etc. 16th c. |
| BIRSE, BIRSS | S. Aberdeenshire 15th c. |
| BISHOP | Edinburgh 15th c., Inverness etc. 17th c. |

| | |
|---|---|
| BISSET, BISSETT | *FRASER*; *GRANT* |
| BLACK | From MACILDUY, *MACGREGOR* |
| | *LAMONT*; *MACLEAN* |
| BLACKADDER | Merse, to Glasgow 15th c., W. Fife 18th c. |
| BLACKBURN | Berwickshire etc. 13th c. |
| BLACKHALL | Aberdeenshire (Garoch) 14th c. |
| BLACKIE | Midlothian etc. 16th c; *LAMONT* |
| BLACKLOCK | Dumfriesshire etc. 17th c. |
| BLACKSTOCK | Dumfriesshire etc. 16th c. |
| BLACKWOOD | Lanarkshire, Perth 16th c. |
| BLAIKIE | From BLAKE |
| BLAIN, BLANE | Wigtownshire 16th c. |
| BLAIR | Ayrshire, Fife, Perthshire 13th c.; |
| | *GRAHAM* of Menteith |
| BLAKE, BLAIK | Berwick 13th c., Ayr 14th c.; *LAMONT* |
| BLANCE, BLANCHE | Shetland 16th c. |
| BLUE | *MACMILLAN* |
| BLYTH, BLYTHE | Berwickshire 13th c., Dundee etc. 15th c. |
| BOA, BOE | Peeblesshire 17th c., from BULLOCK |
| BOAG, BOAK | Stirlingshire, Orkney etc. 16th c. |
| BOATH | Angus (Both) 15th c. |
| BODDIE, BODIE | Roxburghshire 13th c., Aberdeen 15th c. |
| BOGIE | N. Lanarkshire 15th c. |
| BOGLE | Fife, Aberdeen, Edinburgh 14th c. |
| BOLD | Peeblesshire 15th c. |
| BOLT | Shetland 16th c. |
| BOLTON | Lothians 13th c. |
| BONAR, BONNER, BONNAR | Perthshire 12th c., Fife etc. 14th c. *GRAHAM* of Montrose |
| BONE | Ayrshire, Edinburgh 17th c. |
| BONNINGTON | W. Lothian, 15th c. |
| BONNYMAN | Angus etc. 16th c. |
| BONTEIN, BONTINE | From BUNTAIN; *GRAHAM* of Menteith |
| BONTHRON | E. Fife 17th c. |
| BOOG | Same as BOAG |
| BOOKLESS | Melrose 13th c., Lothian 16th c. |
| BOOTH | Aberdeen etc. 13th c. |
| BORLAND | Ayrshire 16th c., Lanarkshire 17th c. |
| BORROWMAN | Angus and Stirlingshire 15th c. |
| BORTHWICK | Roxburghshire and Midlothian 14th c. |
| BOSWALL, BOSWELL | Berwickshire 12th c., Ayrshire, Fife 14th c. |
| BOTHWELL | Lanarkshire 15th c. |
| BOULTON | As BOLTON |
| BOURHILL | Lanarkshire 15th c. |
| BOWDEN | Roxburghshire 13th c. |
| BOWER, BOWERS | Peeblesshire etc. 13th c.; Angus, Aberdeenshire 14th c.; *MACGREGOR* |
| BOWIE | *MACDONALD*; *GRANT* |
| BOWMAKER | E. Lothian etc. 14th c.; *MACGREGOR* |
| BOWMAN | Aberdeen etc. 14th c.; *FARQUHARSON* |
| BOYACK, BOWICK | Fife, Angus etc. 16th c. |
| BOYCE, BOYES | Dumfriesshire etc. 12th c.; *FORBES* |
| BOYD | Ayrshire 13th c.; *STEWART* |
| BOYLE | Galloway 12th c. |
| BOYNE | Banffshire 16th c. |
| BOYTER | E. Fife, Angus 16th c. |

| | |
|---|---|
| BRADLEY | Hawick 13th c. |
| BRAID | Midlothian 12th c. |
| BRAIDWOOD | Lanarkshire 13th c. |
| BRAND | Irvine 14th c., Edinburgh, Angus 16th c. |
| BRASH | E.W. Stirlingshire, Edinburgh 17th c. |
| BREBNER, BREMNER | Ayrshire, Moray etc. 15th c. |
| BRECHIN | Angus 12th c. |
| BREWER | From MACGREWAR, *DRUMMOND* |
| BREWSTER | Lanarkshire 13th c., Aberdeen 14th c., and from MACGREWAR, *FRASER* |
| BRIEVE | *MORRISON* |
| BRIDGEFORD | Kincardineshire 17th c. |
| BRIGGS | Speyside etc. 16th c. |
| BRIMS | Caithness (Thurso) 17th c. |
| BRISBANE | Aberdeenshire, Lennox, Ayrshire 14th c. |
| BROCK | Dunkeld 14th c., Cromarty 16th c. |
| BROCKIE | Angus, Edinburgh 15th c. |
| BRODIE, BRODY | Clan *BRODIE* |
| BRODIE | Kintyre, from Brolochan, *MACDONALD* |
| BROGAN | Aberdeenshire (Slains) 15th c. |
| BROOK, BROOKE | Aberdeen 15th c. |
| BROTCHIE | Caithness, Orkney 17th c. |
| BROTHERSTON | E. Lothian, Lauderdale 12th c. |
| BROUGH | Perthshire and Orkney 16th c. |
| BROUN, BROWN | Lanarkshire, Moray, etc. 13th c., *LAMONT*; *MACMILLAN* |
| BROW | Aberdeen 14th c., Blairgowrie 17th c. |
| BROWNING | Aberdeenshire 14th c. |
| BROWNLEE, BROWNLIE | Lanarkshire etc. 16th c. |
| BRUCE | Clan *BRUCE* |
| BRUNTON | Mid and E. Lothian 14th c. |
| BRYCE, BRICE | Stirling etc. 13th c.; *MACFARLANE* |
| BRYDEN, BRYDON | Roxburghshire 13th c., Selkirk 16th c. |
| BRYDIE, BRYDE | Perthshire 13th c.; *BRODIE* |
| BRYSON | Clydesdale 14th c., Perthshire 15th c. |
| BUCHAN | Buchan etc. 15th c.; *CUMMING* |
| BUCHANAN | Clan *BUCHANAN* |
| BUDGE | MACDONALD, to SINCLAIR, 15th c. |
| BUGLASS | Same as BOOKLESS |
| BUIE | From Macilbowie, see BOWIE |
| BUIST | Fife 16th c., Perthshire 17th c. |
| BULLOCH | Peeblesshire, E. Lothian 13th c. |
| BULLOCK | From BALLOCH, *MACDONALD* |
| BUNCH | Perth 15th c. |
| BUNCLE, BUNKLE | Berwickshire 12th c.; *HOME* |
| BUNTAIN, BUNTING | Peebles 13th c., Lennox 14th c.; *GRAHAM* |
| BUNYAN, BUNZEON | Aberdeen (Cults) to Montrose 17th c. |
| BURDEN, BURDON | Merse 13th c., Perthshire, *LAMONT* |
| BURGESS | Aberdeenshire 14th c., Orkney (from Burgar) 15th c. |
| BURGOYNE, BURGON | Kinross-shire 12th c. |
| BURK | *MACDONALD* |
| BURN | Ayrshire 13th c., Angus etc. 15th c. |
| BURNES, BURNESS | Renfrewshire 14th c., Angus, Ayrshire 16th c.; *CAMPBELL* of Argyll |
| BURNET, BURNETT | Teviotdale 12th c., Deeside 14th c. |

| SURNAME | CLAN OR DISTRICT SOURCE |
|---|---|
| BURNIE | Dumfriesshire, from MACBIRNIE |
| BURNS | From BURNESS |
| BURNSIDE | Angus 16th c., Stirlingshire etc. 17th c. |
| BURRELL, BURREL | Roxburghshire 12th c. |
| BURT | Fife 16th c. |
| BUTCHART, BUTCHER | Angus 15th c.; and from WISHART |
| BUTLER | Midlothian, Perthshire etc. 13th c. |
| BUTTER, BUTTERS | Perthshire 14th c. |
| BUYERS, BYRES | Haddington 14th c.; *LINDSAY* |
| | |
| CABLE | Angus 15th c. |
| CADDELL, CADELL | From Cawder; *CAMPBELL*; also from KETTLE, S.E. Perthshire 17th c. |
| CADENHEAD | N. Selkirkshire 15th c. |
| CADZOW | Lanarkshire (Hamilton) 13th c. |
| CAIE, CAY | Aberdeenshire 16th c. |
| CAIRD | Ayrshire etc. 14th c.; *MACGREGOR* |
| CAIRNCROSS | Angus 14th c. |
| CAIRNS | Mid (Calder) and W. Lothian 14th c. |
| CAITHNESS | S.W. Angus (Kettins) 14th c. |
| CALDER | *CAMPBELL* of Cawdor |
| CALDERHEAD | N.E. Lanarkshire etc. 17th c. |
| CALDERWOOD | Lanarkshire 13th c., Dalkeith 16th c. |
| CALDWELL | Renfrewshire 14th c. |
| CALLAN, CALLEN | From MACALLAN |
| CALLANDER | Perthshire 14th c.; *MACFARLANE* |
| CALLENDAR | *MACGREGOR* |
| CALLUM | *MACGREGOR* |
| CALLUM, CALLAM | From MACCALLUM |
| CALVERT | Angus 15th c., Fife 16th c. |
| CAMPBELL | *CAMPBELL* of Argyll |
| CAMERON | Fife, Angus etc. 13th c.; *CAMERON* |
| CAMBRIDGE | From MACCAMBRIDGE |
| CAMPBELL | Clan *CAMPBELL* of Argyll; of Cawdor of Breadalbane; of Loudoun |
| CAMPBELL of STRACHUR | *MACARTHUR* |
| CANDLISH | From MACCLANDISH |
| CANNAN, CANNON | Galloway 16th c. |
| CANT | W. Fife 14th c., Angus etc. 15th c. |
| CANTLEY, CANTLAY | Aberdeen 15th c. |
| CARGILL | Gowrie 13th c.; *DRUMMOND* |
| CARLYLE, CARLISLE | Dumfriesshire 12th c.; *BRUCE* |
| CARMICHAEL | Lanarkshire 13th c.; *STEWART* Argyll, from MACMICHAEL |
| CARNEGIE | Angus (Balinhard) 14th c. |
| CARNIE | Aberdeenshire 14th c. |
| CARR, CARRE | Same as *KERR* |
| CARRICK | Ayrshire 12th c.; *KENNEDY* |
| CARRIE | From MacHarrie, Ayrshire 15th c. |
| CARRUTHERS | Annandale 13th c.; *BRUCE* |
| CARSE, CARSS | Perth 13th c., Angus etc. 15th c. |
| CARSON | From CORSANE or *MACPHERSON* |
| CARSTAIRS | Lanarkshire 13th c. |
| CARSWELL | Lanarkshire, Roxburghshire 13th c. |
| CARTER | Kelso etc. 15th c. |

| | |
|---|---|
| CASH | From MACCASH |
| CASKEY, CASKIE | *MACLEOD* of Lewis |
| CASSELS | Lanarkshire etc. 17th c. |
| CASSILLIS | Carrick 16th c.; *KENNEDY* |
| CASSIE | Lanark 14th c., Aberdeen etc. 15th c. |
| CATHAL, CATHIL | *MACDONALD* |
| CATHCART | Renfrewshire 12th c. |
| CATHIE | *MACFIE* |
| CATANACH | *CLAN CHATTAN*; *MACPHERSON* |
| CATTELL | From CADDELL |
| CATTO | Aberdeenshire 15th c. |
| CAVEN | E. Kirkcudbrightshire (Cavens) 15th c. |
| CAVERS | Roxburghshire etc. 15th c.; *DOUGLAS* |
| CAW | From MACCAW, *STUART* |
| CESSFORD | Roxburghshire 16th c.; *KERR* |
| CHALMERS | Ayrshire etc. 12th c.; Aberdeenshire, *CAMERON* |
| CHAMBERS | Lanarkshire etc. 13th c.; *CAMERON* |
| CHAPLIN | Aberdeenshire etc. 13th c. |
| CHAPMAN | Lanarkshire, Aberdeen etc. 14th c. |
| CHARLES, CHARLESON | From MACKERLICH, *MACKENZIE* |
| CHARTERS | Dumfriesshire 12th c. |
| CHEAPE, CHEAP | Perth 16th c., Stirling, Kinross 17th c. |
| CHERRY, CHERRIE | Ayr 14th c. |
| CHEYNE, CHIENE | *CUMMING*; *SUTHERLAND* |
| CHIRNSIDE | Berwickshire 13th c. |
| CHISHOLM | Clan *CHISHOLM* |
| CHRISTIE, CHRISTY, CHRISTISON | Fife etc. 15th c.; *FARQUHARSON* |
| CHRYSTAL | Ayrshire, Buchan 15th c. |
| CLAPPERTON | Stirling 16th c., Stewartry 17th c. |
| CLARK | *MACGREGOR* |
| CLARK, CLARKE | *CLAN CHATTAN*; *CAMERON* *MACINTOSH*; *MACPHERSON* |
| CLARKSON, CLEARY | As CLARK, from MACCHLERY |
| CLAY | From MACLAY, Appin *STEWART* |
| CLEGHORN | Lanark 16th c. |
| CLELAND, CLELLAND | Hamilton 13th c.; *MACNAB* |
| CLEMENT | S. Perthshire etc. 15th c.; *LAMONT* |
| CLEPHANE | Lauderdale 12th c., Fife 13th c. |
| CLERK | Midlothian 12th c.; and as CLARK |
| CLINKSCALES | Berwickshire (Coldingham) 17th c. |
| CLOUSTON | Orkney (Stromness) 15th c. |
| CLOW, CLOWE | Strathearn (Clow) 16th c. |
| CLUNESS, CLUNIES | Beauly 14th c.; *MACKENZIE* |
| CLUNIE, CLUNY | Gowrie 13th c.; *MACPHERSON* |
| CLYNE | *SUTHERLAND*; *SINCLAIR* |
| COATES, COATS | From COUTTS |
| COBB | Angus 15th c.; *LINDSAY* |
| COCHRANE, COCHRAN | Paisley 13th c.; also MACEACHRAN |
| COCKBURN, COBURN | Merse, to Roxburgh etc. 13th c. |
| COGLE, COGHILL | Caithness (Wick) 17th c. |
| COLES | Galloway; *MACDOUGALL* |
| COLL | *MACDONALD* |
| COLLEDGE | Hawick etc. 17th c. |
| COLLIE, COLLEY | Aberdeenshire 13th c. |
| COLLIER, COLYEAR | Fife 16th c.; *ROBERTSON* |

| SURNAME | CLAN OR DISTRICT SOURCE |
|---|---|
| COLLINS | Angus, Aberdeen 15th c. |
| COLLISON | Aberdeen 15th c. |
| COLMAN | *BUCHANAN* |
| COLQUHOUN | Clan *COLQUHOUN* |
| COLSON | *MACDONALD* |
| COLTART, COLTHERS | Galloway 12th c. |
| COLVILLE, COLVIN | Roxburghshire, Ayrshire 12th c. |
| COMBE, COMBICH | *MACTHOMAS*; *MACINTOSH* |
| COMBIE, COMBY | Perthshire etc., Appin *STEWART* |
| COMMON, COMMONS | Dumfriesshire; *CUMMING* |
| COMRIE | Perthshire 15th c.; *MACGREGOR* |
| CONACHER | *MACDOUGALL*, to *STEWART* |
| CONDIE | Strathearn (Condie) 15th c. |
| CONLEY, CONLAY | From MACDONLEAVY |
| CONN | Aberdeenshire, *MACDONALD* |
| CONNAL, CONNELL | *MACDONALD* |
| CONNON | From CONN, *GORDON* |
| CONNOCHIE, CONOCHIE | See MACCONOCHIE |
| CONSTABLE | Lanarkshire 15th c.; *HAY* |
| COOK, COOKE | Berwickshire etc. 12th c.; *MACDONALD* |
| COOPER, COWPER | Fife (Cupar) etc. 13th c. |
| COPLAND, COPELAND | Merse 12th c., Orkney, Shetland 15th c. |
| CORBET, CORBETT | Teviotdale 12th c.; *ROSS* |
| CORDINER | Aberdeen etc. 15th c. |
| CORMACK | From MACCORMACK, *BUCHANAN* |
| CORRIE, CORRY | Dumfriesshire 12th c., Ayrshire 13th c. |
| CORRIGALL | Orkney (Harray) 15th c. |
| CORSANE, CORSON | Galloway 12th c. |
| CORSTORPHINE | Edinburgh, to E. Fife 16th c. |
| COSSAR | Lanarkshire, Berwickshire 14th c. |
| COTTON | Fife etc. 17th c. |
| COULL | Aberdeenshire 13th c.; *MACDONALD* |
| COULSON | *MACDONALD* |
| COULTER | Lanarkshire, Aberdeenshire 13th c. |
| COULTHARD | See COLTART |
| COUPER, COUPAR | Fife (Cupar) etc. 13th c. |
| COUSIN | Aberdeen 16th c., Fife 17th c. |
| COUSLAND | Dalkeith 13th c.; *BUCHANAN* |
| COUSTON | S.W. Angus (Couston) etc. 16th c. |
| COUTIE, COUTTIE | S.W. Angus 17th c. |
| COUTTS | Aberdeenshire 14th c.; *FARQUHARSON* Angus 14th c.; *MACDONALD* |
| COVENTRY | Berwick 13th c., Angus 14th c. |
| COWAN, COWEN | From MACCOWAN: also *COLQUHOUN* |
| COWE | Midlothian etc. 14th c. |
| COWIE | Mearns etc. 14th c.; *FRASER* |
| CRABB, CRABBE | Aberdeen, Berwick 14th c. |
| CRAE | From *MACRAE* |
| CRAIG | Midlothian etc. 13th c.; *GORDON* |
| CRAIGDALLIE | *MACGREGOR* |
| CRAIGIE | W. Lothian 12th c., Orkney 14th c. |
| CRAIGMYLE | Deeside (Craigmile) 16th c. |
| CRAIK | Dumfriesshire etc. 13th c. |
| CRAMB, CRAM | S.W. Fife (Crombie) 12th c., Perthshire 13th c. |
| CRAMOND | Edinburgh, to Angus 13th c. |

| | |
| --- | --- |
| CRANE, CRAN | Angus 13th c., Aberdeenshire 14th c. |
| CRANSTON | Midlothian, Roxburghshire 12th c. |
| CRAW | E. Berwickshire (Auchincraw) 14th c. |
| CRAWFORD | Upper Clydesdale 12th c.; *LINDSAY* |
| CREE | Ayrshire, from *MACRAE* |
| CRERAR, CREARER | From 'SIVEWRIGHT'; *MACINTOSH*; |
| | also *MACGREGOR* |
| CRIBBES | Lanarkshire, W. Lothian 13th c. |
| CRICHTON, CRIGHTON | Midlothian (Crichton) 11th c.; Perthshire 19th c. |
| | (now a clan in its own right) |
| CRIRIE | Galloway, *MACDONALD* |
| CROALL, CROLL | Kincardineshire 13th c. |
| CROCKETT, CROCKET | N. Lanarkshire 13th c., Angus etc. 15th c. |
| CROMAR | Mar (Cromar), *FARQUHARSON* |
| CROMARTY | To Orkney, 16th c., *MACKENZIE* |
| CROMB | As CRUM; *MACDONALD* to *GORDON* |
| CROMBIE | See CRAMB; Aberdeen 16th c.; *GORDON* |
| CROOK, CROOKES | Renfrewshire (Crookston) 12th c. |
| CROSBIE | Dumfriesshire 12th c.; *BRUCE* |
| CROW, CROWE, CROY | Perthshire etc. 15th c.; *ROSS* |
| CROWTHER | *MACGREGOR* |
| CROZER, CROSIER | Liddesdale 14th c.; *ARMSTRONG* |
| CRUDEN | Aberdeenshire 15th c. |
| CRUICKSHANK ⎫ | E. Lothian 13th c. |
| CRUICKSHANKS ⎬ | Aberdeen etc. 15th c. |
| CRUIKSHANK etc. ⎭ | *STEWART* of Atholl |
| CRUM, CROOM | Benderloch, *MACDONALD* |
| CRYSTAL, CRYSTALL | See CHRYSTAL |
| CUBBISON | Stewartry of Kirkcudbright 17th c. |
| CUBIE, CUBBIE | Angus 15th c. |
| CULBERT | Angus, Fife 16th c. |
| CULCHONE | From *COLQUHOUN* |
| CULLEN | Banffshire 14th c.; *GORDON* |
| CULLOCH | From MACCULLOCH |
| CUMMING, CUMMIN, | Clan *CUMMING* |
| CUMMINGS, CUMYNS | |
| CUNINGHAME, etc. | See CUNNINGHAM |
| CUNNINGHAM | N. Ayrshire 12th c. |
| CUNNISON | *ROBERTSON*; *MACFARLANE* |
| CURLE | Ayrshire 14th c. |
| CURRER, CURROR | Berwickshire 13th c., Perth 15th c. |
| CURRIE, CURREY | Annandale 12th c.; and MACVURRICH |
| CURSITER | Orkney (Cursetter) 16th c. |
| CUTHBERT | Lothian, Angus, Inverness 15th c. |
| CUTHBERTSON | Lothian, Angus, Aberdeen 15th c. |
| CUTHILL, CUTHELL | E. Lothian (Preston) 16th c. |
| CUTLER | Berwickshire etc. 15th c. |
| | |
| DACKER, DACRE | Aberdeen 15th c. |
| DAKERS | Angus (Brechin) 16th c. |
| DALGARNO | Nithsdale to Aberdeenshire 16th c. |
| DALGETTY | Fife, Angus 16th c. |
| DALGLEISH | Ettrickdale (Dalgleish) 15th c. |
| DALLAS | Moray 13th c., *MACINTOSH* |
| DALRYMPLE | Kyle (Dalrymple) 13th c. |
| DALTON | Dumfriesshire, Aberdeen 14th c. |

| SURNAME | CLAN OR DISTRICT SOURCE |
|---|---|
| DALZIEL, DALYELL | Motherwell 13th c., Shetland 'from Yell' |
| DANIEL, DANIELS | From DONALD, *MACDONALD* |
| DARG, DARGE | E. Lothian 15th c.; *GORDON* |
| DARLING | Tweedside and Midlothian 14th c. |
| DARROCH, DARRACH | Stirlingshire 15th c.; Renfrewshire 17th c.; *MACDONALD* (now a clan in its own right) |
| DAVIDSON | Clan *DAVIDSON*; *CLAN CHATTAN* |
| DAVIE, DAVEY | Aberdeen 15th c.; *DAVIDSON* |
| DAVIS, DAVISON, DAWSON | Same as DAVIDSON |
| DAY, DEA, DEY | Banffshire 16th c.; *DAVIDSON* |
| DEAN, DEANE | Ayrshire 15th c.; *DAVIDSON* |
| DEANS | Hawick and Glasgow 16th c. |
| DEAS, DEASON | From *DAVIDSON* |
| DEMPSTER | Perthshire 13th c., Angus etc. 14th c. |
| DENHOLM, DENHAM | Roxburghshire 13th c. |
| DENNIS | Aberdeen 15th c., Linlithgow 16th c. |
| DENNISON | From DENNISTON; also DENSON |
| DENNISTON | Renfrewshire 13th c.; *STEWART* |
| DENNY | Stirlingshire 15th c. |
| DENOON, DENUNE | Dunoon 13th c.; *CAMPBELL*; *ROSS* |
| DENSON | Perthshire; *MACGREGOR* |
| DENTON | Dumfriesshire 13th c. |
| DESSON | From DAVIDSON |
| DEUCHAR, DEUCHARS | Angus 13th c.; *LINDSAY* |
| DEWAR | *MACNAB*; also from MACINDEOR |
| DICK | Ayrshire etc. 15th c. |
| DICKIE | Lanarkshire etc. 16th c. |
| DICKSON, DICKISON | Upper Clyde etc. 14th c.; *KEITH* |
| DINGWALL | *MUNRO*; *ROSS* |
| DINSMORE | From DUNSMORE, *MURRAY* |
| DINWIDDIE, DINWOODIE | Annandale (Dinwoodie) 13th c.; *MAXWELL* |
| DIS, DISE | Same as DYCE |
| DISHART | Fife 15th c. |
| DISHINGTON | Angus 14th c., Fife 15th c. |
| DIXON, DIXSON | From DICKSON |
| DOBBIE, DOBIE | Peebles etc. 15th c.; *ROBERTSON* |
| DOBBIN, DOBBINSON | Ayrshire 15th c.; *ROBERTSON* |
| DOBSON, DOBIESON | Lanarkshire 15th c.; *ROBERTSON* |
| DOCHART, DOCHERTY | Perthshire; *MACGREGOR* |
| DODD, DODDS, DODS | Fife 13th c., E. Lothian, Sutherland 15th c. |
| DOIG, DOCK | S. Perthshire, *DRUMMOND* |
| DOLES | *MACINTOSH* |
| DOLLAR | Clackmannanshire (Dollar) 14th c. |
| DON | Aberdeenshire, Perthshire 16th c. |
| DONACHIE, DONAGHY | See MACCONACHIE |
| DONALD, DONALDSON | *MACDONALD* |
| DONAT, DONNAT | Perthshire 15th c. |
| DONLEVY | *STEWART* of Appin |
| DUNNACHIE | See MACCONACHIE |
| DONNELL, DONNELSON | *MACDONALD* |
| DORREN, DORAN | Kirkcudbright 17th c. |
| DORWARD, DORRAT | Mar etc. 13th c., Angus 15th c.; *GORDON* |
| DOTT | Fife 15th c., from DODD |

| | |
|---|---|
| DOUGAL, DOUGALL, | *MACDOUGALL* |
| DOUGAN, DOUGHAN | Galloway etc. 17th c. |
| DOUGHTIE, DOUGHTY | Peeblesshire 14th c. |
| DOUGLAS, DOUGLASS | Clan *DOUGLAS* |
| | Argyllshire, from MACLUCAS |
| DOULL | 'Donald', Caithness 17th c.; also DOUGAL |
| DOVE, DOW | *BUCHANAN*; *DAVIDSON* |
| DOWALL, DOWELL | Galloway; *MACDOUGALL* |
| DOWIE | From MACILDOWIE |
| DOWNIE | Angus 14th c.; *LINDSAY* |
| DRAIN | From MACDRAIN |
| DRENNAN, DRINNAN | Stranraer etc. 17th c. |
| DREVER | Orkney 15th c. |
| DREW | Stirlingshire, Glasgow 16th c. |
| DRIMMIE | Gowrie (Drimmie); *MURRAY* |
| DRUM | Deeside (Drum) 14th c. |
| DRUMMOND | Clan *DRUMMOND*; Stranraer, from DRENNAN |
| DRYBURGH | Berwickshire 13th c. |
| DRYDEN | Angus 13th c. |
| DRYSDALE | Annandale 15th c., to Fife 16th c.; *DOUGLAS* |
| DUDGEON | E. Lothian 16th c. |
| DUFF | *MACDUFF*; *GORDON* |
| DUFFIE, DUFFY | *MACFIE* |
| DUFFUS, DUFFES | Moray 13th c.; *SUTHERLAND* |
| DUGAL, DUGALD | *MACDOUGALL* |
| DUGUID, DUCAT | Perth etc. 14th c., Aberdeenshire 15th c. |
| DUILACH | *STEWART* of Atholl |
| DUNBAR | E. Lothian 11th c., Moray etc. 14th c.; |
| | HOME; *MURRAY* |
| DUNCAN, DUNCANSON | Berwick etc. 14th c.; *ROBERTSON* |
| DUNDAS | W. Lothian 12th c. |
| DUNLOP, DUNLAP | N. Ayrshire (Dunlop) 13th c. |
| DUNN, DUN, DUNNE | Moray, Peeblesshire etc. 13th c. |
| DONNACHIE | *ROBERTSON* |
| DUNNEL | *MACDONALD* |
| DUNNET, DUNNETT | N. Caithness 16th c. |
| DUNS, DUNSE | Berwickshire (Duns) 12th c. |
| DUNSIRE | E. Lanarkshire (Dunsyre) 13th c. |
| DUNSMORE, | N. Fife (Dunsmore) 13th c.; *MURRAY* |
| DUNSMURE | |
| DURHAM | Dumfriesshire, Angus etc. 13th c. |
| DURIE | Fife (Leven) 13th c. |
| DURWARD | Same as DORWARD |
| DUTHIE | Perthshire, Mearns 16th c.; *ROSS* |
| DYCE, DYAS | Aberdeen (Dyce) 15th c.; *SKENE* |
| DYE, DYSON | *DAVIDSON* |
| DYER | Aberdeen etc. 14th c. |
| DYKES | Lanarkshire, Perthshire 16th c. |
| | |
| EADIE | Same as ADDIE; *GORDON* |
| EANRIG, EANRUIG | *GUNN* |
| EASDALE, etc. | See ISDALE |
| EASON, EASSON | *MACKINTOSH* of Glentilt |
| EASTON | Peeblesshire 13th c. |
| EATON | From AYTON |
| ECCLES | Berwickshire 12th c., Dumfriesshire 14th c. |

| | |
|---|---|
| ECKFORD | Teviotdale (Eckford) 13th c. |
| EDGAR | Nithsdale 12th c. |
| EDIE, EDDIE | Same as ADDIE; *GORDON* |
| EDINGTON | E. Berwickshire 12th c. |
| EDISON | Same as ADDISON; *GORDON* |
| EDMISTON | From EDMONSTON |
| EDMOND, EDMUNDS | Aberdeen 15th c., Stirling 16th c. |
| EDMONSTON | Midlothian 13th c., Roxburghshire 14th c. |
| EDWARD, EDWARDS, EDWARDSON | From 'Udward'; Dumbarton and Edinburgh 15th c. |
| EGGIE, EGGO | Mar 14th c.; *MACINTOSH* |
| ELDER | Aberdeen etc. 15th c.; *MACINTOSH* |
| ELLIOT, ELIOTT | Clan *ELLIOT* |
| ELLIS, ELLISON | Berwickshire 13th c., Dundee 15th c.; *MACPHERSON* |
| ELMSLIE, EMSLIE | Aberdeenshire 13th c. |
| ELPHINSTONE | E. Lothian 13th c. |
| ENRICK | 'Eanrig', Henry: *GUNN* |
| ERASMUSON | Shetland 17th c. |
| ERSKINE | Renfrewshire 13th c., Dryburgh 16th c. |
| ESPLIN | Stirling, Angus etc. 16th c. |
| ESSLEMONT | Ythanside; *GORDON* |
| ESSON | *MACINTOSH* of Glentilt |
| EUNSON, EWENSON | Perthshire 13th c., Orkney 17th c.; and from MACEWAN |
| EWAN | See MACEWAN |
| EWART | Roxburghshire, Galloway 16th c. |
| EWEN, EWING | See MACEWAN |
| EWER, EWERS | See URE |
| FAED | Galloway; *MACLAREN* |
| FAICHNEY | Perthshire 16th c. |
| FAIR | Border 15th c.; *ROSS* |
| FAIRBAIRN | Lothian, Fife 12th c.; *ARMSTRONG* |
| FAIRFOUL | Fife 15th c. |
| FAIRGRIEVE | Tweedside 17th c. |
| FAIRHOLM, FERME | Lanarkshire, Edinburgh 17th c. |
| FAIRIE, FARIE | Ayrshire 13th c., Rutherglen 14th c. |
| FAIRLEY, FAIRLIE | Ayrshire, Midlothian 14th c.; *ROSE* |
| FAIRWEATHER | Perthshire 15th c., Angus 16th c. |
| FALCONER | Kincardineshire 13th c.; *KEITH* |
| FARMER | Fife 14th c., Perth 15th c. |
| FARNINGTON | Roxburghshire (Fairnington), 13th c. |
| FARQUHAR | Ayrshire 14th c.; *FARQUHARSON* |
| FARQUHARSON | Clan *FARQUHARSON*; *CLAN CHATTAN* |
| FAULDS | Leith 15th c., Glasgow 16th c. |
| FEDERITH | *SUTHERLAND* |
| FEE | *MACFIE* |
| FENDER | Edinburgh 16th c., Aberdeen 17th c. |
| FENTON | E. Lothian, Angus 13th c.; *CHISHOLM* |
| FENWICK | Roxburghshire 13th c., Ayr 14th c. |
| FERGUS, FERGIE | *FERGUSON* |
| FERGUSON, FERGUSSON | Clan *FERGUSON* |
| FERNIE, FERNEY | Cupar-Fife 14th c. |
| FERRIER | E. Lothian and Angus 13th c. |
| FERRIES | *FERGUSON*; *FARQUHARSON* |

| SURNAME | CLAN OR DISTRICT SOURCE |
|---|---|
| FERSEN | *MACPHERSON* |
| FIDDES, FETTES | Kincardineshire 13th c., Angus 15th c. |
| FIDDLER, FIDLER | Lanark 15th c., Stirling etc. 16th c |
| FIFE | Fife 13th c., Aberdeen 15th c.; *MACDUFF* |
| FINDLATER | Banffshire 14th c.; *OGILVIE* |
| FINDLAY, FINDLAYSON, FINLAY, FINLAISON, FINLAYSON | *FARQUHARSON* |
| FINNIE, FINNEY | Aberdeen, Glasgow etc. 16th c. |
| FISHER | Perthshire 13th c., *CAMPBELL*; *MACGREGOR* |
| FISKEN | Perthshire 16th c. |
| FLAWS | Orkney 15th c. |
| FLEMING | Lanarkshire etc. 12th c.; *MURRAY* |
| FLETCHER | Roxburgh and Angus 14th c.; *MACGREGOR* |
| FLETT | Orkney 15th c. |
| FLINT | Berwickshire etc. 17th c. |
| FLOCKHART, FLUCKER | Fife 13th c. |
| FOGGO, FOGO | Merse 12th c.; Aberdeen, Foggie |
| FOOT, FOOTE | Angus 15th c. |
| FORBES | Clan *FORBES* |
| FORD, FOORD | Annandale etc. 15th c. |
| FORDYCE | Banffshire 15th c.; *FORBES* |
| FOREST | Tweeddale etc. 14th c.; *DOUGLAS* |
| FORGIE | *FERGUSON* |
| FORMAN, FOREMAN | Midlothian 13th c., Tweedside 15th c. |
| FORREST | From FOREST, also FORRESTER |
| FORRESTER | Stirlingshire 12th c.; *MACDONALD* |
| FORSON | Melrose 17th c. |
| FORSTER, FOSTER | From FORRESTER |
| FORSYTH | Edinburgh, Stirling 14th c.; *LAMONT* |
| FORTUNE | E. Lothian 13th c. |
| FOTHERINGHAM | Angus 13th c.; *LINDSAY* |
| FOUBISTER | Orkney 16th c. |
| FOULIS, FOWLIS | Perthshire etc. 13th c.; *MUNRO* |
| FOWLER | Berwickshire, Edinburgh 14th c. |
| FOX | Kelso 16th c., Angus 17th c. |
| FRAME, FRAM | N. Lanarkshire etc. 15th c. |
| FRANCIS, FRANCE | Dumfriesshire 12th c.; *STEWART* |
| FRASER, FRAZER | Clan *FRASER* |
| FRATER | Kelso 16th c. |
| FREEMAN | Peeblesshire 13th c. |
| FRENCH | Annandale, Lothian etc. 13th c. |
| FRESER, FREZEL | Same as *FRASER* |
| FREW | S. Perthshire 16th c. |
| FRIER, FREER | Berwickshire etc. 13th c. |
| FRISELL, FRIZELLE | Same as *FRASER* |
| FULLARTON, FULLERTON | Ayrshire 13th c.; *STUART* of Bute |
| FULTON | Ayrshire, Lanarkshire 13th c. |
| FURMAGE | Dundee 13th c. |
| FUTHIE | Angus, Aberdeen 14th c.; *OGILVIE* |
| FYALL | Fife 16th c. |
| FYFE, FYFFE | See FIFE |
| GAIR | E. Ross 16th c.; *GAYRE*; *ROSS*; *MACGREGOR* |
| GAIRN, GAIRNS | Angus, from GARDEN; also *GAYRE* |

| SURNAME | CLAN OR DISTRICT SOURCE |
|---|---|
| GALBRAITH<br>GALBREATH } | Lennox 12th c.<br>*MACFARLANE*; *MACDONALD* |
| GALL, GAUL | See GALT |
| GALLETLY | Perth, Aberdeen 13th c. |
| GALLIE | Ayrshire 15th c.; *GUNN* |
| GALLOWAY | To Atholl 13th c.; *MACFARLANE* |
| GALT | Perth 14th c., Aberdeen 15th c., Ayrshire 17th c.;<br>*MACDONALD* |
| GANSON, GAUNSON | Nairn 13th c.; *GUNN* |
| GARDEN, GARDYNE | Angus and Midlothian 13th c. |
| GARDINER, GARDNER | Perthshire etc. 15th c.; *GORDON* |
| GARLAND | Perthshire 13th c. |
| GARIOCH, GARRICK,<br>  GARRIOCK, GERRIE | Aberdeenshire, Midlothian 13th c.,<br>  Shetland 15th c.; *GORDON* |
| GARRATT, GARRETT | Glasgow 16th c., from GERARD |
| GARRISON, GARSON | *GAYRE* |
| GARROW | Perthshire, see MACGARROW |
| GARVIE | Gowrie, Angus 16th c.; MACGARVIE |
| GAULD, GAULT | Same as GALT |
| GAULDIE, GALDIE | Same as GALLIE |
| GAVIN, GAVINE | Angus, Border etc. 17th c. |
| GAY | Angus 15th c., Fife etc. 17th c. |
| GAYRE | Clan *GAYRE* |
| GEAR | Shetland 17th c., from GAIR; *GAYRE*; *ROSS* |
| GEDDES | *ROSE*, to *SCOTT* 15th c.; *GORDON* |
| GEDDIE | Angus (Glamis) 14th c. |
| GEEKIE, GEIKIE | S. Angus (Gagie) 15th c. |
| GEIR | *GAYRE* |
| GELLATLY | Perth, Aberdeen 13th c. |
| GEMMELL | E. Lothian, Tweed 13th c., Carrick 16th c. |
| GEORGE | Ayrshire 15th c. |
| GEORGESON | Angus 15th c.; *GUNN* |
| GERARD, GERRARD | Annandale 12th c., Aberdeenshire 16th c. |
| GIBB, GIBBON | From GILBERT |
| GIBSON | Fife, Midlothian 13th c.; *BUCHANAN*;<br>  *CAMERON* |
| GIFFORD | E. Lothian 12th c.; *HAY* |
| GILBERT | Bute etc. 14th c., *BUCHANAN* |
| GILBERTSON | Peeblesshire 13th c.; *BUCHANAN*; *CAMERON* |
| GILBRIDE | *MACDONALD* |
| GILCHRIST | *MACLACHLAN*; *OGILVIE* |
| GILES | Lanarkshire 13th c., Dunbartonshire 16th c. |
| GILFILLAN | Stirlingshire, *MACNAB* |
| GILL | Perth etc. 14th c.; *MACDONALD* |
| GILLAM | 'William', S. Perthshire 17th c. |
| GILLAN, GILLAND | From GILLIAN; also GILLILAND |
| GILLANDERS | Kincardineshire 13th c.; *ROSS* |
| GILLESPIE | Lennox 12th c.; *MACPHERSON* |
| GILLIAN, GILLON | 'Gil'lan'; *MACLEAN* |
| GILLIES, GILLIE | Lothian 12th c.; *MACPHERSON* |
| GILLILAND | From MACLELLAND; Ayrshire 17th c. |
| GILMORE, GILMOUR | Clackmannan etc. 12th c.; *MORRISON* |
| GILRAY, GILVRAY | From *MACGILLIVRAY* |
| GILROY | From MACILROY |
| GILRUTH | From MACILRIACH; *FRASER* |
| GILZEAN | From GILLIAN, *MACLEAN* |

| SURNAME | CLAN OR DISTRICT SOURCE |
|---|---|
| GIRDWOOD | Lanarkshire (Carnwarth) 16th c. |
| GLADSTONE | Clydesdale 13th c., Teviotdale 14th c. |
| GLAISTER | Angus (Glaister) 13th c. |
| GLASS | Bute etc. 15th c.; *STUART* of Bute |
| GLASSFORD | Mid Lanarkshire 13th c. |
| GLEGG | Angus and Mearns 17th c. |
| GLEN | Peeblesshire (Traquair) 14th c. |
| GLENDINNING | E. Dumfriesshire 13th c.; *DOUGLAS* |
| GLENNIE, GLENNY | Braemar 14th c., *MACINTOSH* |
| GLOAG | Perthshire 16th c. |
| GLOVER | Perth 13th c., Glasgow etc. 16th c. |
| GOLD, GOOLD | Angus 13th c. |
| GOLDIE | Galloway etc. 16th c. |
| GOLLAN | Kinross-shire 13th c. |
| GOOD | Ayr, Glasgow etc. 16th c. |
| GOODAL | Roxburghshire 13th c. |
| GOODFELLOW | Angus 15th c., Lanark etc. 17th c. |
| GOODLAD, GOODLET | Stirling 14th c., Fife 15th c., Shetland 16th c. |
| GOODSIR, GOODYEAR | E. Fife 14th c.; also *MACGREGOR* |
| GOODWILLIE | Fife 12th c. |
| GORDON | Clan *GORDON* |
| GORRIE, GORRY | Perthshire 16th c.; *MACDONALD* |
| GOUDIE, GOULDIE | Edinburgh, Shetland, Ayrshire 16th c.; *MACPHERSON* |
| GOULD | Perthshire 17th c., from GOLD |
| GOURLAY, GOURLEY | Midlothian, Fife etc. 12th c. |
| GOVAN | Glasgow, to Peeblesshire 13th c. |
| GOW | Fife etc. 16th c.; *MACPHERSON* |
| GOWAN, GOWANS | *MACDONALD*; Perthshire, *MACPHERSON* |
| GRACIE | From GREUSACH via Grassick |
| GRAHAM, GRAHAME | Clan *GRAHAM* |
| GRAINGER, GRANGER | Roxburgh, Edinburgh etc. 13th c. |
| GRANT | Clan *GRANT* |
| GRASSICK | From GREUSACH |
| GRAY | Fife etc. 13th c.; *SUTHERLAND* From MACGLASHAN, *STEWART* |
| GREEN | Roxburghshire 13th c., Moray etc. 15th c. |
| GREENLAW | Berwickshire 12th c.; *HOME* |
| GREENLEES | Lanarkshire (Cambuslang) 16th c. |
| GREER | *MACGREGOR* |
| GREGG | *MACGREGOR* |
| GREGOR, GREGORY | Fife 14th c.; *MACGREGOR* |
| GREGORSON, GREGSON | *MACGREGOR* |
| GREIG | Fife 13th c.; *MACGREGOR* |
| GREUSACH | Aberdeenshire; *FARQUHARSON* |
| GREWAR | See MACGREWAR |
| GREY | Same as GRAY |
| GREYSON | From GRIERSON; *MACGREGOR* |
| GRIERSON, GRIER | Dumfriesshire 14th c.; *MACGREGOR* |
| GRIESCK | *MACFARLANE* |
| GRIEVE, GREIVE | Berwickshire 13th c., Aberdeen etc. 14th c. |
| GRIFFIN | Angus and Moray 13th c. |
| CRIGG | *MACGREGOR* |
| GRIGOR | Aberdeenshire etc.; *MACGREGOR* |
| GRIMMOND | Perthshire, from MACCRIMMON |
| GRINTON | Peeblesshire, W. Lothian 16th c. |

| | |
|---|---|
| GROAT | Caithness 15th c.; *SINCLAIR* |
| GROUNDWATER | Orkney 17th c. |
| GROZIER | From CROSIER; *ARMSTRONG* |
| GRUAMACH | *MACFARLANE* |
| GRUAR, GRUER | See MACGREWAR |
| GRUBB | Angus (Brechin) 17th c. |
| GUDGER | *MACGREGOR* |
| GUILD | Stirling, Angus, Perthshire 15th c. |
| GUINNESS | *MACGREGOR* |
| GULLAND, GULLEN | E. Lothian (Gullane) 12th c. |
| GUNN | Clan *GUNN* |
| GUTHRIE | Angus (Guthrie) 13th c. |
| | |
| HADDEN, HADDON | Kelso, to Perthshire 12th c.; *GRAHAM* |
| HADDOW | Lanarkshire etc. 17th c. |
| HAGGART, HAGART | Perthshire 16th c.; *ROSS* |
| HAIG | Berwickshire 12th c. |
| HAIR, HARE | Ayrshire, Edinburgh 14th c. |
| HALCROW | Orkney 15th c. |
| HALDANE, HALDEN | Same as HADDEN |
| HALKETT, HACKETT | Ayrshire and Fife 13th c. |
| HALIBURTON | Merse 12th c., to Angus 13th c.; *HOME* |
| HALL | Renfrewshire and Fife 14th c. |
| HALLEY, HALLY | Orkney 16th c., Perthshire 17th c. |
| HALLIDAY | Dumfriesshire 14th c. |
| HAMILTON | Renfrewshire 13th c. |
| HANDYSIDE | Berwick 14th c. |
| HANNAH, HANNAY | Wigtownshire 13th c. |
| HANNAN | Kirkcudbrightshire 17th c. |
| HANNING | Berwick 12th c., Dumfriesshire etc. 17th c. |
| HARCUS | Merse (Harcarse) 13th c., Orkney 16th c. |
| HARDIE, HARDY | Lanarkshire 13th c., and MACHARDIE |
| HARKESS, HARKES | Same as HARCUS |
| HARKNESS | Dumfriesshire 16th c. |
| HARPER | Lanarkshire etc. 13th c.; *BUCHANAN* |
| HARPERSON | From MACCHRUITER |
| HARRISON | Aberdeen 14th c., Fife 15th c., Shetland 17th c. |
| HARROLD, HAROLD | Orkney 15th c., *MACLEOD* |
| HARROWER | E. Fife 14th c., Perth etc. 15th c. |
| HART, HARTE | Lanarkshire 13th c. |
| HARVEY, HARVIE | Aberdeen etc. 14th c.; *KEITH* |
| HASTIE | Menteith 14th c., Border 16th c. |
| HASTINGS | N.E. Angus (Dun) 12th c. |
| HASTON | Galloway (Heston I.) 17th c. |
| HASWELL | Berwickshire 12th c. |
| HAWES, HAWS | *CAMPBELL* |
| HAWSON | Tweedside 15th c.; *CAMPBELL* |
| HAWICK | Roxburghshire 12th c. |
| HAWTHORN | Galloway 15th c.; *MACDONALD* |
| HAXTON | Mearns (Halkerston) 13th c.; *KEITH* |
| HAY | Clan *HAY* |
| HEATLIE, HEATLY | Tweedside 13th c. |
| HEDDELL, HEDDLE | Orkney 14th c. |
| HEDDERWICK | Dunbar 15th c.; also Arbroath 16th c. |
| HEGGIE | From MACKEGGIE; *MACINTOSH* |

| SURNAME | CLAN OR DISTRICT SOURCE |
|---|---|
| HENDERSON | Aberdeen and Liddesdale 14th c.; *GUNN* From MACHENRY |
| HENDRIE, HENDRY, HENRY, HENDERY | Ayrshire etc. 16th c.; and from MACHENRY |
| HEPBURN | E. Lothian 14th c. |
| HERBERT | Stirlingshire 13th c. |
| HERBERTSON | Glasgow and E. Lothian 16th c. |
| HERD | Angus and Galloway 14th c. |
| HERDMAN | Aberdeenshire etc. 15th c. |
| HERIOT, HERRIOT | Midlothian 12th c., to Glasgow etc. 16th c. |
| HERKES, HERKIS | Same as HARCUS |
| HERMISTON | Roxburghshire 12th c., to E. Ross etc. 14th c. |
| HERON | Stewartry 12th c.; also MACKERRON |
| HERRIES | Dumfriesshire 13th c., Galloway 14th c. |
| HERVEY | Same as HARVEY |
| HEWISON | *MACDONALD* |
| HEWITT, HEWAT | Aberdeen 15th c., Berwickshire 17th c. |
| HIGGINSON | From MACKEGGIE; *MACINTOSH* |
| HIGHET, HIGHGATE | Glasgow 16th c. |
| HILL | Roxburghshire 13th c., Aberdeen etc. 14th c. |
| HISLOP, HESLOP | Edinburgh and Lanarkshire 15th c. |
| HOBKIRK | Hawick (Hopekirk), to Midlothian 16th c. |
| HOBSON | *ROBERTSON* |
| HODGE, HODGES | From ROGER; Glasgow etc. 15th c. |
| HOGARTH, HOGGART | Fife 15th c., Roxburghshire 17th c. |
| HOGG, HOG, HOGGE | Berwickshire, Edinburgh etc. 13th c. |
| HOLLAND | Orkney, Angus, Ayrshire 15th c. |
| HOLLIDAY | From HALLIDAY |
| HOLMES | Ayrshire 15th c.; and from *HOME* |
| HOME | Clan *HOME* |
| HONEYMAN | Fife 15th c., Orkney 17th c. |
| HOOD | Midlothian and Moray, 13th c. |
| HOOK | Dumfriesshire 13th c. |
| HOPE | Lanarkshire etc. 13th c., Lothian 16th c. |
| HOPKIRK | See HOBKIRK |
| HORN, HORNE | Dumfriesshire 14th c., Aberdeen etc. 15th c. |
| HORNER | Angus 15th c., Glasgow 16th c. |
| HORSBURGH | Peebles 13th c. |
| HOSSACK, HOSICK | Beauly Firth 16th c.; *MACINTOSH* |
| HOULISTON | Midlothian (Heriot) 13th c. |
| HOUSTON, HOUSTOUN | Renfrewshire 12th c.; *MACDONALD* Caithness, from OGSTOUN |
| HOWATT, HOWITT | Aberdeen 15th c., Angus 17th c.; *MACDONALD* |
| HOWDEN | Same as HADDEN |
| HOWE, HOW, HOWIE | Angus and Ayrshire 16th c.; *MACDONALD* |
| HOWELL, HOWELLS | From MACHOWELL, *MACDOUGALL* |
| HOWIESON, HUGHSON | Aberdeenshire etc. 14th c.; *MACDONALD* |
| HOY | Roxburghshire, Orkney 17th c. |
| HUDSON, HUTSON | Kelso 15th c.; also from HUTCHON |
| HUGGAN | Fife, Lauderdale 16th c.; Bute 17th c. |
| HUIE | From MACILDOWIE, *MACLEAN* |
| HUME | Same as *HOME*; *MACDUFF* |
| HUNNAM, HOUNAM | E. Roxburghshire (Hownam) 12th c. |
| HUNTER, HUNT | Peeblesshire, Ayrshire etc. 13th c., Stronsay (Hunto) 16th c.; *STUART* |
| HUNTLY | Berwickshire 13th c.; *GORDON* |

| | |
|---|---|
| HURRY, HURRIE | Kincardineshire (Urrie) 13th c.; *KEITH* |
| HUSBAND | Nairn 13th c., Perth 16th c. |
| HUTCHEON, HUTCHIN | See HUTCHON |
| HUTCHESON, HUTCHINSON, HUTCHISON | Glasgow, Aberdeen etc. 15th c.; *MACDONALD* |
| HUTCHON, HUTSON | Aberdeen etc. 15th c.; *MACDONALD* |
| HUTTON | Lanark 13th c., Fife 15th c. |
| HYND, HYNDE | Glasgow etc. 15th c. |
| HYNDFORD | Lanark 13th c. |
| HYNDMAN | Renfrewshire 16th c. |
| HYSLOP | See HISLOP |
| | |
| IMLACH, IMLAH | Aberdeenshire 15th c. |
| IMRIE, IMERY | S. Perthshire 15th c., Fife 16th c. |
| INCH | W. Fife 13th c., Angus 15th c.; *INNES* |
| INCHES | Perthshire; *ROBERTSON* |
| INGLIS, INGLES | Lanarkshire etc. 13th c.; *DOUGLAS* |
| INGRAM | Angus 14th c.; *COLQUHOUN* |
| INKSTER | Orkney 15th c., Shetland 16th c. |
| INNES | Clan *INNES* |
| INRIG | Caithness 17th c., see ENDRICK |
| INVERARITY | Angus 17th c. |
| IRELAND | Perthshire 13th c., Orkney 14th c. |
| IRONS | Angus 15th c. |
| IRONSIDE | Aberdeenshire 16th c. |
| IRVINE, IRVING, IRWIN, IRVIN | Dumfriesshire, Ayrshire 12th c.; Deeside 14th c., Shetland 16th c. |
| ISAAC, ISAACS | See MACISAAC |
| ISBISTER | Orkney (Harray) 16th c. |
| ISDALE, EASDALE | Border 'Eskdale' to Ayrshire 15th c. |
| ISLES | *MACDONALD* |
| IVERACH, IVORY | From MACIVER, *MACKENZIE* |
| IVERSON | Same as MACIVER |
| IZATT, IZZETT | W. Fife, Ayrshire 16th c. |
| | |
| JACK | Angus and Lanarkshire 15th c. |
| JACKSON | Aberdeen, Glasgow etc. 15th c. |
| JACOB, JACOBS | Angus 14th c. |
| JAFFREY | Aberdeenshire 16th c., from JEFFREY |
| JAMESON, JAMIESON | *GUNN*; (Maccamie); *STUART* |
| JAMIE | W. Lothian 16th c., Lanarkshire etc. 17th c. |
| JARDINE | Angus 12th c., Dumfriesshire 13th c. |
| JARVIS, JARVIE | Angus, Stirling etc. 16th c. |
| JEFFERIES, JEFFERS, JEFFERSON, JEFFERY | From 'Geoffrey', Peeblesshire etc. 13th c., Angus, Aberdeen 14th c.; *MACDONALD* |
| JENKIN, JENKINS | Moray, Lanarkshire etc. 16th c. |
| JERRAT, JARRETT | See GARRATT |
| JENNER | Berwickshire 13th c., Inverness 15th c. |
| JERDAN | From JARDINE |
| JERVIS | From 'Gervase', see JARVIS |
| JESSIMAN | Aberdeenshire 16th c.; *GORDON* |
| JOBSON, JOPSON | Annandale 14th c., Edinburgh etc. 17th c. |
| JOHNSON | *GUNN*; also from MACIAN |
| JOHNSTON | Clan *JOHNSTON*; also *MACGREGOR* |

| SURNAME | CLAN OR DISTRICT SOURCE |
|---|---|
| JOHNSTONE | As *JOHNSTON*; Coll, *MACDONALD* of Ardnamurchan |
| JOLLIE, JOLLY | Kincardineshire 14th c. |
| JOPP | Perth 14th c., Huntly 16th c.; *GORDON* |
| JORDAN | Aberdeen 13th c. |
| JOSS | Fife 14th c., Aberdeenshire 16th c. |
| JUDGE | Perthshire 13th c.; *MORRISON* |
| JUDSON | Edinburgh 14th c. |
| JUNER, JUNOR | Inverness, from JENNER |
| JUSTICE | Perthshire and Angus 15th c. |
| KAY, KEAY | Aberdeen etc. 14th c.; *DAVIDSON* From MACKAY |
| KEAN, KEENE | From MACIAN |
| KEDDIE | Fife etc. 16th c., from MACADIE |
| KEEGAN | From MACKEEGAN, *MACDONALD* |
| KEIGHREN | From MACEACHRAN |
| KEILLER, KEILOR | Angus, Perth, Mar 13th c. |
| KEIR | Stirlingshire 13th c., Ayrshire 16th c. |
| KEITH | Clan *KEITH* *MACPHERSON*; *SUTHERLAND* |
| KELDAY | Orkney (Keldall) 16th c. |
| KELLAR, KELLER | From KEILLER; also MACKELLAR |
| KELLAS | Moray, *FARQUHARSON* |
| KELLOCK | Stirling 14th c., Fife 15th c. |
| KELLY, KELLIE | Galloway 12th c., Angus 14th c.; *MACDONALD* |
| KELMAN | Aberdeenshire 16th c. |
| KELTIE, KELTY | Callander (Keltic), to Edinburgh 17th c. |
| KEMP | Edinburgh 15th c., Dingwall 16th c. |
| KENNAWAY | Fife (Kennoway), to W. Lothian 17th c. |
| KENNEDY | Clan *KENNEDY*; Lochaber, *CAMERON* |
| KENNETH, KENNETHSON | *MACKENZIE* |
| KENRICK, KENDRICK | From MACKENDRICK |
| KENT | E. Lothian 12th c., Fife 16th c. |
| KEPPIE | Fife 17th c. |
| KER, KERR | Clan *KERR* |
| KERMACK | Buchan (Kermuck) 14th c. |
| KERRACHER | MACERRACHER, *FARQUHARSON* |
| KESSAN, KESSEN | Lennox 14th c., Ayr etc. 16th c. |
| KETCHEN, KETCHIN | *MACDONALD* of Clanranald |
| KETTLE, KETTLES | S.E. Perthshire 13th c. |
| KEY, KEYS | Same as KAY |
| KID, KIDD | Lanarkshire 12th c., Angus 14th c. |
| KIDDIE | Same as KEDDIE |
| KILGOUR | N.W. Fife, to Aberdeen 16th c.; *MACDUFF* |
| KILPATRICK | Same as KIRKPATRICK |
| KINCAID | S. Stirlingshire (Kincaid) 15th c. (now a clan in its own right) |
| KING | Aberdeenshire 13th c., Berwickshire etc. 15th c.; and from MACAREE |
| KINGHORN | Fife, to Lothian etc. 13th c. |
| KININMONTH | Fife 12th c. |
| KINLOCH | N.W. Fife (Kinloch-Rossie) 12th c. |
| KINNAIRD | Perthshire (Gowrie) 12th c. |
| KINNEAR | Fife (Wormit) 12th c. |

| | |
|---|---|
| KINNELL | Angus 14th c.; Fife 17th c.; *MACDONALD* |
| KINNIESON | See CUNNISON |
| KINROSS | Kinross 12th c. |
| KIRK | Perth, Arbroath 15th c., Dumfriesshire 17th c. |
| KIRKALDY | Fife (Kirkcaldy) 17th c. |
| KIRKBY | Berwickshire 13th c. |
| KIRKLAND | Merse 13th c., Glasgow etc. 15th c. |
| KIRKNESS | Orkney 14th c., Shetland 15th c. |
| KIRKPATRICK | Nith 12th c.; *DOUGLAS*; *COLQUHOUN* |
| KIRKWOOD | Stirling 15th c., Ayrshire 16th c.; *MACGREGOR* |
| KISSACK, KISSOCK | Moray, from MACISAAC |
| KNIGHT | Angus 14th c., Dumfries etc. 16th c. |
| KNOWLES, KNOX | Aberdeenshire (Deer) 15th c. |
| KNOX | Renfrewshire 13th c.; *MACFARLANE* |
| KYD, KYDD | Same as KIDD |
| KYLE | Ayrshire (Kyle) 15th c. |
| KYNOCH | *ROBERTSON*; *MACKENZIE* |
| | |
| LACHLAN, LACHIE | *MACLACHLAN* |
| LACKIE | Angus, from LECKIE |
| LAIDLAW, LAIDLAY | Selkirkshire 13th c.; *SCOTT* |
| LAIKIE | *MACGREGOR* |
| LAING | Dumfries 14th c., Glasgow 15th c.; *GORDON*; *COLQUHOUN*; *MACDONALD* |
| LAIRD | Berwick and Peeblesshire 13th c. |
| LAMB | Merse 13th c., Leith etc. 14th c.; *LAMONT* |
| LAMBERT | E. Fife 13th c. |
| LAMBIE, LAMMIE | From LAMB, Angus 13th c.; *LAMONT* |
| LAMONDSON | *LAMONT* |
| LAMONT, LAMOND | Clan *LAMONT* |
| LANDALE, LANDELLS, LANDELS | Roxburghshire, E. Lothian 12th c.; *HOME* |
| LANE | Angus, Aberdeen 16th c. |
| LANG | Berwickshire 13th c., Aberdeen 14th c.; *GORDON*; *MACDONALD* |
| LANGLANDS | Peeblesshire 14th c.; *SCOTT* |
| LARNACH | Lorne, to Caithness etc.; *MACLAREN* |
| LARNACK | Lorne, to *STEWART* of Atholl |
| LATIMER | Dumfriesshire 14th c. |
| LATTA, LATTO | Ayrshire (Laithes) 14th c. |
| LAUCHLAN | *MACLACHLAN* |
| LAUDER | Lauderdale 13th c. |
| LAURENCE | Biggar 13th c., Aberdeen 16th c.; *MACLAREN* |
| LAURENSON | Fife 15th c., Shetland 16th c.; *MACLAREN* |
| LAURIE | Galloway etc. 16th c.; *GORDON* |
| LAW | Glasgow etc. 15th c.; *MACLAREN* |
| LAWRENCE, LAWRIE | See LAURENCE, LAURIE |
| LAWSON | Midlothian 14th c.; *MACLAREN* |
| LAWTHER | See LAUDER |
| LEACH | See LEITCH |
| LEADBETTER | W. Lothian 14th c. |
| LEAN | From *MACLEAN* |
| LEAPER | Edinburgh 12th c., Buchan 13th c.; NAPIER |
| LEARMONTH | Berwickshire (Earlston) 11th c. |
| LEARY | From MACLEARY |
| LEASK | Buchan (Leask) 14th c., Orkney 15th c. |

| SURNAME | CLAN OR DISTRICT SOURCE |
|---|---|
| LEAVY | From MACDONLEAVY |
| LEAY | From MACLEAY |
| LECKIE, LECKY | Stirlingshire 14th c.; *MACGREGOR* |
| LEDINGHAM | Aberdeenshire 16th c. |
| LEE | Lanark 12th c. |
| LEES, LEESON | From MACLEES |
| LEGG, LEGGE | Dumfriesshire 13th c., Banffshire 16th c. |
| LEGGAT, LEGGET | Stirling etc. 15th c. |
| LEIGHTON | Fife and Angus 13th c. |
| LEIPER, LEIPPER | See LEAPER |
| LEISHMAN | Lanarkshire 15th c., Stirlingshire 16th c. |
| LEISK | Same as LEASK |
| LEITCH, LEETCH | Aberdeen, Glasgow etc. 14th c.; *MACBETH*; *MACDONALD* |
| LEITH | Lothian and Aberdeenshire 14th c. |
| LEITHEAD | Midlothian and Border 17th c. |
| LEMMON, LEMOND | From LAMONT |
| LENG | From LANG |
| LENNIE, LENNY | Perthshire (Leny) 13th c.; *BUCHANAN* |
| LENNOX | Lennox 12th c.; *MACFARLANE* |
| LENNOX | *STEWART* |
| LESLIE, LESSLIE | Clan *LESLIE* |
| LESSELS | 'Lascelles', Fife etc. 12th c. |
| LETHAM, LETHEM | Berwickshire and Angus 13th c. |
| LEUCHARS, LEURS | Fife (Leuchars) 14th c. |
| LEVACK | Caithness 17th c.; Appin *STEWART* |
| LEWIS | Bute, *STUART*; *MACLEOD* |
| LIDDELL, LIDDLE | Roxburghshire 13th c., Aberdeen 14th c. |
| LIGHTBODY | N. Lanarkshire 16th c., W. Lothian 17th c. |
| LILBURN | Aberdeen 15th c. |
| LILLICO | Roxburghshire 17th c. |
| LILLIE, LILLY | Peeblesshire 13th c. |
| LIMOND, LIMONT | From *LAMONT* |
| LIND, LINE | From LYNN |
| LINDORES | Fife, Aberdeen etc. 15th c. |
| LINDSAY | Clan *LINDSAY* |
| LINKLATER | Orkney 15th c. |
| LILLE, LILE | Same as LYLE |
| LISTER | From LITSTER |
| LISTON | W. Lothian (Liston) 12th c. |
| LITHGOW | Linlithgow, to Berwick etc. 13th c. |
| LITSTER | Perth, Lothians etc. 13th c. |
| LITTLE | Angus 13th c., to Dumfriesshire etc. 14th c. |
| LITTLEJOHN | Aberdeen and Glasgow 15th c. |
| LIVINGSTON, LIVINGSTONE | W. Lothian 12th c.; From MACLEAY; Appin *STEWART*; *MACDOUGALL* |
| LOBBAN | Nairn 16th c.; *MACLENNAN* |
| LOCH | Peeblesshire 13th c. |
| LOCHHEAD | Lanarkshire, Aberdeenshire 13th c. |
| LOCKE, LOCK | Roxburghshire 13th c., Glasgow etc. 16th c. |
| LOCKERBY | Lockerbie (place), *DOUGLAS* |
| LOCKHART | Ayrshire, Lanarkshire 12th c. |
| LOCKIE | Angus and Midlothian 16th c. |
| LOGAN | Ayrshire, Fife etc. 13th c.; *MACLENNAN* |
| LOGIE, LOGGIE | Fife etc. 13th c. |
| LONGMUIR | Ayrshire and Midlothian 13th c. |

| SURNAME | CLAN OR DISTRICT SOURCE |
|---------|------------------------|
| LONIE | From MACGILLONIE, *CAMERON* |
| LORIMER | Perthshire 12th c., Midlothian 15th c. |
| LORNE | Appin *STEWART*; *CAMPBELL* |
| LORNIE | Gowrie 13th c., *HAY* |
| LORRAINE | Berwickshire 13th c. |
| LOTHIAN | Lothian, Berwick 14th c., Angus etc. 15th c. |
| LOUDEN, LOUDON | Ayrshire (Loudoun) 12th c.; *CAMPBELL* Fife 16th c. (from LOTHIAN) |
| LOURIE, LOWRIE | Same as LAURIE |
| LOUTIT, LOUTTIT | Strathearn 12th c., to Orkney 15th c. |
| LOVE | Dundee 13th c., Glasgow 15th c.; *MACKINNON* |
| LOVEL, LOVELL | Roxburghshire 12th c., Angus 13th c. |
| LOW, LOWE | Perthshire 14th c., Angus 15th c.; *MACLAREN* |
| LOWDEN, LOWDON | See LOUDEN |
| LOWSON | Aberdeen 14th c.; *MACLAREN* |
| LOY | From MACCLOY, *STUART* |
| LUCAS, LUCKIE | From MACLUCAS |
| LUGTON | Midlothian, to Fife 16th c. |
| LUKE, LUCK | From MACLUCAS, *LAMONT* |
| LUMBARD, LOMBARD | Renfrewshire 13th c.; *STEWART* |
| LUMGAIR | Kincardineshire 13th c.; *KEITH* |
| LUMLEY | Lanark 14th c. |
| LUMSDEN ⎫ LUMSDAINE ⎭ | Berwickshire 12th c., Fife 14th c. Aberdeenshire 14th c.; *FORBES* |
| LUNAN | Angus and Aberdeenshire 14th c. |
| LUNDIE, LUNDIN | Fife and Angus 12th c. |
| LUNN, LUND | Berwickshire, Angus etc. 16th c. |
| LYALL, LYELL | Angus 14th c.; *SINCLAIR* |
| LYLE | Renfrewshire 12th c.; *STEWART* |
| LYNE, LYNN | Ayrshire and Perth 13th c. |
| LYON | Perthshire 12th c.; *FARQUHARSON* |
| | |
| MABEN, MABON | Dumfriesshire etc. 17th c. |
| MACACHIN | *MACDONALD* of Clanranald |
| MACACHOUNICH | *COLQUHOUN* |
| MACADAM | Angus 15th c., Ayrshire 16th c.; *MACGREGOR* |
| MACADIE | *FERGUSON*; *MUNRO* |
| MACAICHAN | *MACDONALD* of Clanranald |
| MACADOO | Galloway 17th c. |
| MACAINDRA | *MACFARLANE* |
| MACAINSH | See MACANISH |
| MACALASTER | (Same as FLETCHER), *MACGREGOR* |
| MACALDONICH | *BUCHANAN* |
| MACALDOWIE, MACALDUIE | See MACILDOWIE |
| MACALEAR | Galloway, from MACCLURE |
| MACALEERIE | Galloway, from MACCHLERY |
| MACALEES | Galloway, from MACLEES |
| MACALESTER | *MACALISTER*; *MACGREGOR* |
| MACALISTER | Clan *MACALISTER* |
| MACALL | See MACCALL |
| MACALLAN | Aberdeenshire 17th c., *MACFARLANE* Clanranald *MACDONALD*; *GRANT* *MACKAY*; Kirkcudbrightshire 14th c. |
| MACALLASTER | *MACALISTER* |
| MACALLEY | From *MACAULAY* |

26

| | |
|---|---|
| MACALLISTER | *MACALISTER* |
| MACALLUM | From *MACCALLUM* |
| MACALMAN | From MACCALMAN, *BUCHANAN* |
| MACALONIE | From MACGILLONIE, *CAMERON* |
| MACALPIN, MACALPINE | Clan *ALPIN* |
| MACANDIE | (Bernera) Harris *MACLEOD* |
| MACANDREW | *ROSS*; Inverness, *MACINTOSH* |
| MACANGUS } | Argyll, Galloway, *MACINNES* |
| MACANISH } | Atholl, *MACGREGOR* |
| MACARA, MACAREE | Perthshire, *MACGREGOR* |
| MACARA, MACARRA | Wester Ross, *MACRAE* |
| MACARTHUR | Clan *MACARTHUR* |
| | Skye, *MACDONALD* |
| MACARTNEY | See MACCARTNEY |
| MACASKIE | Galloway, from MAGASKILL |
| MACASKILL | *MACLEOD* of Lewis |
| MACASLAN, MACASLIN | *BUCHANAN* |
| MACAULAY | *MACAULAY*; Clan *ALPIN* |
| MACAULLY | *MACLEOD* of Lewis |
| MACAUSELAN, MACAUSLAN, MACAUSLAND, MACAUSLANE | *BUCHANAN* |
| MACAWEENEY | Same as MACWHINNIE |
| MACAY | *SHAW* |
| MACBAIN | *MACKAY*; *MACBEAN* |
| MACBAXTER | *MACMILLAN* |
| MACBAY, MACBEY | *MACLEAN* of Duart |
| MACBEAN | *MACBEAN* |
| MACBEATH | Same as *MACBETH* |
| MACBEOLAIN | *MACKENZIE* |
| MACBETH } | *MACBETH*; *MACBEAN* |
| MACBHEATH } | *MACDONALD*; *MACLEAN* |
| MACBIRNIE | Galloway 15th c.; *MATHESON* |
| MACBLAIN | Dumfries 12th c., Wigtownshire etc. 15th c. |
| MACBRAIR | Dumfriesshire 15th c. |
| MACBRAYNE | *MACNAUGHTON*; *MACDONALD* |
| MACBRIDE | Moray, Bute 14th c.; *MACDONALD* |
| MACBRIEVE | *MORRISON* |
| MACBRYDE | See MACBRIDE |
| MACBURIE | *MACDONALD* of Clanranald |
| MACBURNIE | Same as MACBIRNIE |
| MACCAA | Galloway, from *MACKAY* |
| MACCABE | Arran, *MACLEOD* of Lewis |
| MACCAFFER | Islay, *MACDONALD* |
| MACCAFFIE | From MACGUFFIE |
| MACCAIG | Galloway 15th c.; *MACLEOD* of Harris; *FARQUHARSON* |
| MACCAINSH | From MACANGUS |
| MACCAIRN | 'MacCiaran', see MACKERRON |
| MACCAIRTER | Same as *MACARTHUR* |
| MACCAISH | See MACCASH |
| MACCALL | Nithsdale, Bute 15th c.; *MACAULAY* |
| MACCALLUM | *MACLEOD* of Lewis, to *MALCOLM* |
| MACCALMAN | MACCOLMAN, *BUCHANAN* |

| SURNAME | CLAN OR DISTRICT SOURCE |
|---|---|
| MACCALMONT | Ayr 16th c., from MACCOLMAN |
| MACCAMBRIDGE | 'MacAmbrose', *MACDONALD* |
| MACCAMIE | FULLARTON, to Bute *STUART* |
| MACCAMMOND | Galloway 17th c., from MACCOLMAN |
| MACCANCE | From MACANGUS |
| MACCANDLISH | Galloway 17th c. |
| MACCANNELL | Islay etc. from *MACDONALD* |
| MACCANSH | From MACANGUS |
| MACCARDNEY | Same as MACHARDIE |
| MACCARRON | 'MacLaren', see MACKERRON |
| MACCARTAIR,<br>  MACCARTER | Same as *MACARTHUR* |
| MACCARTNEY | Galloway 16th c.; and MACHARDIE |
| MACCASH | Perthshire, from MACTAVISH |
| MACCASKIE | Galloway, from MACASKILL |
| MACCASKILL | *MACLEOD* of Lewis |
| MACCASLAND | *BUCHANAN* |
| MACCATHIE | Galloway 15th c.; *MACFIE* |
| MACCAULEY | *MACAULAY* |
| MACCAUSE | Perthshire, Ayrshire 15th c.; MACTAVISH |
| MACCAW | From *MACKAY*; Bute, to *STUART* |
| MACCAY | See *MACKAY* |
| MACCHEYNE | Galloway and Cowall 17th c. |
| MACCHLERY | *CLAN CHATTAN: CAMERON*;<br>  *MACINTOSH*; *MACPHERSON* |
| MACCHRUITER | Carrick 14th c.; *BUCHANAN* |
| MACCLAIR | From MACCHLERY |
| MACCLANE | From *MACLEAN* |
| MACCLARENCE | *MACLAREN* |
| MACCLAY | From MACLEAY |
| MACCLEAN | Ayrshire, *MACLEAN* |
| MACCLEARY | From MACCHLERY |
| MACCLEAY | *STEWART* of Appin |
| MACCLEISH | See MACLEISH |
| MACCLELLAND | From MACLELLAN |
| MACCLEMENT | *LAMONT* |
| MACCLINTOCK | See MACLINTOCK |
| MACCLORY | Galloway 17th c. |
| MACCLOY | See MACLOY |
| MACCLUNG | Galloway 17th c. |
| MACCLURE | Galloway 16th c.; Harris *MACLEOD* |
| MACCLUSKIE | Kintyre etc.; *MACDONALD* |
| MACCLYMONT | Ayrshire 17th c.; *LAMONT* |
| MACCODRUM | North Uist, *MACDONALD* |
| MACCOLL | *MACDONALD* to Appin *STEWART* |
| MACCOLM | Same as MACCOMBE |
| MACCOLMAN | Ayrshire 12th c.; *BUCHANAN* |
| MACCOMAS | Same as MACOMISH |
| MACCOMB,<br>  MACCOMBIE,<br>  MACCOMIE | Clan *MACTHOMAS* |
| MACCOMBE | Galloway 16th c., Appin *STEWART*;<br>  *MACTHOMAS* |
| MACCOMBICH }<br>MACCOMBIE }<br>MACCOMIE } | *STEWART* of Appin<br>Angus, *MACTHOMAS*;<br>  *MACINTOSH* |

| | |
|---|---|
| MACCONACHER | *MACDOUGALL* |
| MACCONACHIE | Atholl, Bute, *ROBERTSON* |
| | Argyll *CAMPBELL*; *MACGREGOR* |
| MACCONCHER | Lorne, *MACDOUGALL* |
| MACCONCHIE | *MACFARLANE* |
| MACCONDACH | See MACCONACHIE; *MACINTOSH* |
| MACCONDOCHIE | *MACFARLANE*; *MACGREGOR* |
| MACCONDY | MACCONACHIE, *MACGREGOR* |
| MACCONICH | *ROBERTSON* |
| MACCONNACH | *MACKENZIE*; *ROBERTSON* |
| MACCONNAL | See MACCONNELL |
| MACCONNECHY | See MACCONACHIE |
| MACCONNELL | S.W. Scotland, from *MACDONALD* |
| MACCONOCHIE | See MACCONACHIE |
| MACCOISH | *MACFIE*, to *MACDONALD* |
| MACCOOK | Kintyre etc., *MACDONALD* |
| MACCORKILL | *GUNN*; Argyll, Lewis *MACLEOD* |
| MACCORKINDALE | See MACCORQUODALE |
| MACCORKLE | See MACCORKILL |
| MACCORMACK | Galloway 17th c.; *BUCHANAN* |
| MACCORMICK | MACLAINE of Lochbuie |
| MACCORQUODALE | Argyll 15th c.; *MACLEOD* of Lewis |
| MACCORRY | *MACQUARRIE* |
| MACCOSH | Ayrshire 16th c. |
| MACCOSHAM | *MACINTYRE*; Skye, *MACDONALD* |
| MACCOUL | From *MACDOUGALL* |
| MACCOURT | Wigtownshire 15th c., Carrick 16th c. |
| MACCOWAN | *MACDONNELL* of Glengarry, to |
| | *MACDOUGALL*; and from *COLQUHOUN* |
| MACCOWATT | From MACWATT, *FORBES* |
| MACCOWELL | From MACDOWELL |
| MACCOYLE | Perthshire, from *MACDOUGALL* |
| MACCRA, MACCRACH | Ayrshire etc. 17th c.; *MACRAE* |
| MACCRACKEN | Galloway 16th c.; *MACNAUGHTON* |
| MACCRAE, MACCREA | See MACCRA |
| MACCRAIN, MACCRAN | Jura, Islay, *MACDONALD* |
| MACCRAITH | See MACRAITH |
| MACCRAW, MACCRAY | From *MACRAE* |
| MACCREADIE | Galloway 17th c. |
| MACCREATH | From *MACRAE* |
| MACCREE, MACCRIE | Ayrshire 16th c.; *MACRAE* |
| MACCRIMMON | Skye, *MACLEOD* of Harris |
| MACCRINDLE | Galloway 15th c.; *MACDONALD* of Clanranald |
| MACCRIRIE | Dumfriesshire 15th c.; *MACDONALD* |
| MACCRONE | Galloway etc. 16th c. |
| MACCRORIE | See MACRORIE |
| MACCHROSTIE | Perthshire 16th c. |
| MACCROUTHER | Same as MACGREWAR |
| MACCROW, MACCROY | From *MACRAE* |
| MACCRUITER | *MACGREGOR* |
| MACCRUM | Benderloch, *MACDONALD* |
| MACCUAIG | Islay, *MACDONALD*; *MACLEOD* of Harris, |
| | *FARQUHARSON* |
| MACCUBBIN, | MACGIBBON, Dumfriesshire etc. 14th c.; |
| MACCUBBING | *BUCHANAN* |
| MACCUBIE | MACGIBBON, Jedburgh 17th c.; *BUCHANAN* |

| SURNAME | CLAN OR DISTRICT SOURCE |
| --- | --- |
| MACCUISH | *MACFIE* to *MACDONALD* |
| MACCUITHEIN | Skye 17th c.; *MACDONALD* |
| MACCULLAGH | See MACCULLOCH |
| MACCULLIE | MACCULLOCH; Banffshire, *GUNN* |
| MACCULLOCH | Galloway, Stewartry 11th c.; Argyll, E. Ross, from MacCullich |
| MACCUNE, MACCUNN | Galloway 14th c.; from MACEWAN |
| MACCURDY | Same as MACKIRDY |
| MACCURE | From MACIVER |
| MACCURRACH, MACCURRIE | From MACVURRICH |
| MACCUTCHEN, MACCUTCHEON | *MACDONALD* |
| MACDADE, MACDAID | Same as *DAVIDSON* |
| MACDAIRMID | *CAMPBELL* |
| MACDANIELL | From *MACDONALD* |
| MACDAVID | *DAVIDSON* |
| MACDERMID | *CAMPBELL* |
| MACDERMONT | *CAMPBELL*, Galloway |
| MACDIARMID | *CAMPBELL* |
| MACDILL | Ayrshire 16th c.; *MACDOUGALL* |
| MACDONACHIE | Same as MACCONNACHIE |
| MACDONALD | Clan *MACDONALD* of the Isles<br>*MACDONALD* of Clanranald<br>of Ardnamurchan; of Glencoe |
| MACDONELL | Clan *MACDONELL* of Glengarry;<br>Clan *MACDONELL* of Keppoch |
| MACDONLEAVY | Same as MACCLEAY |
| MACDOOL, MACDOUL, MACDOUALL | Galloway, *MACDOUGALL* |
| MACDOUGAL, MACDOUGALL | Clan *MACDOUGALL*<br>also *MACGREGOR* |
| MACDOWALL, MACDOWELL | Galloway, *MACDOUGALL* |
| MACDRAIN | Kintyre, *MACDONALD* |
| MACDUFF | Clan *MACDUFF*; Clan *ALPIN* |
| MACDUFFIE | *MACFIE* |
| MACDUGALD | *MACDOUGALL* |
| MACEACHAN, MACEACHEN | Carrick, Wigtown 13th c.; *MACDONALD* of Clanranald |
| MACEACHERN | Kintyre, *MACDONALD* |
| MACEACHIN | See MACEACHAN |
| MACEACHRAN | Same as MACEACHERN |
| MACEARACHER | Same as MACERRACHER |
| MACEDDIE | Inverness, *MUNRO* |
| MACELEARY | Galloway, from MACCHLERY |
| MACELFRISH | *MACDONALD* |
| MACELHERAN | 'MacCiaran' see MACKERRON |
| MACELLAR | MACKELLAR, *CAMPBELL* of Argyll |
| MACELVIE | MACKELVIE, *CAMPBELL* of Argyll |
| MACERCHAR, MACERRACHER | Argyll, *LAMONT*; *MACFARLANE*<br>Perthshire; *FARQUHARSON* |
| MACEUR, MACEVER | Galloway, from MACIVER |
| MACEWAN, MACEWEN | Cowal, Galloway, *MACLACHLAN*<br>Lorne, Perthshire, *MACDOUGALL* |
| MACEWING | Galloway, *MACLACHLAN* |

| SURNAME | CLAN OR DISTRICT SOURCE |
|---|---|
| MACFADDEN | See MACFADYEN |
| MACFADYEN, MACFADZEAN | Mull, *MACLAINE* of Lochbuie; to Galloway etc. 15th c. |
| MACFAIL, MACFALL | From MACPHAIL, *MACINTOSH* |
| MACFAIT, MACFADE | See MACFEAT |
| MACFARLAN, MACFARLANE | Clan *MACFARLANE* |
| MACFARQUHAR | Same as MACERCHAR |
| MACFATER | See MACPHATER |
| MACFAULD | From MACPHAIL |
| MACFAYDEN | From MACFADYEN |
| MACFEAT, MACFEAD | *MACLAREN* |
| MACFEE | Same as *MACFIE* |
| MACFERGUS | Lennox 16th c.; *FERGUSON* |
| MACFIE | *MACFIE*; Clan *ALPIN* |
| MACFETRIDGE | *MACLEAN*, to Ayrshire 16th c. |
| MACGAA | Galloway, from MACKAY |
| MACGACHAN | From MACEACHAN |
| MACGAIR | *GAYRE* |
| MACGARROW | Perthshire 16th c; *STEWART* |
| MACGARVIE | Wigtownshire 15th c. |
| MACGAW | Galloway, from *MACKAY* |
| MACGEACH | *MACGREGOR* |
| MACGEACHAN | From MACEACHAN |
| MACGEACHY, MACGECHIE | *MACDONALD* |
| MACGEE | See MACGHEE |
| MACGEOCH | Wigtownshire 15th c.; *MACFARLANE* |
| MACGEORGE | Galloway etc. 16th c.; from DEWAR |
| MACGHEE, MACGHIE | Dumfries etc. 13th c.; *MACKAY* |
| MACGIBBON | *BUCHANAN*; *CAMPBELL* *GRAHAM* of Menteith |
| MACGILCHRIST | *MACLACHLAN*; *OGILVIE* |
| MACGILL | Galloway 13th c.; *MACDONALD* |
| MACGILLECHALLUM | *MACLEOD* of Raasay |
| MACGILLEDOW | *LAMONT* |
| MACGILLERY | *CAMERON* |
| MACGILLIES | Perthshire 12th c.; *MACPHERSON* |
| MACGILLAVANTIC | *MACDONNELL* of Keppoch |
| MACGILLIVRAY | Clan *MACGILLIVRAY*; Clan *CHATTAN* *MACLAINE* of Lochbuie |
| MACGILLONIE | *CAMERON* |
| MACGILP | From MACKILLOP |
| MACGILROY | *GRANT*; *MACGILLIVRAY* |
| MACGILVERNOCK | Argyll, *GRAHAM* of Menteith |
| MACGILVRA, MACGILVRAY | See *MACGILLIVRAY* |
| MACGIRR | Galloway, Stewartry 17th c. |
| MACGLASHAN, MACGLASHEN | Clan *CHATTAN: MACINTOSH* Atholl *STEWART*, to *ROBERTSON* |
| MACGLASHRICH | MACIVER, *CAMPBELL* *MACDONNELL* of Keppoch |
| MACGORRIE, MACGORRY | *MACDONALD* Cowal, *LAMONT*; *MACQUARRIE* |
| MACGOUGAN | Kintyre, *MACNEILL* of Gigha |
| MACGOUN, MACGOW | See MACGOWAN |

| | |
| --- | --- |
| MACGOWAN, MACGOWN | *MACDONALD*; *MACPHERSON* Nithsdale 14th c. |
| MACGRAIL | From *MACNEIL* |
| MACGRAIN | Galloway, from MACCRAIN |
| MACGRATH, MACGRAW | From *MACRAE* |
| MACGREGOR | Clan *MACGREGOR*; Clan *ALPIN* |
| MACGREUSICH | *BUCHANAN*; *MACFARLANE* |
| MACGREWAR | *DRUMMOND*; *MACGREGOR* Beauly Firth, *FRASER* |
| MACGRIGOR | *MACGREGOR* |
| MACGRIME | *GRAHAM* of Menteith |
| MACGRORY | *MACLAREN* |
| MACGROUTHER, MACGRUDER, MACGREUER, MACGRUTHER | Same as MACGREWAR |
| MACGRUMEN | *MACGREGOR* |
| MACGUARIE | *MACQUARRIE* |
| MACGUBBIN | From MACGIBBON |
| MACGUFFIE | From MACGUFFOCK: also *MACFIE* |
| MACGUFFOCK | Galloway 13th c., Aberdeen 14th c.; *DOUGLAS* |
| MACGUGAN, MACGUIGAN | Kintyre, *MACNEILL* of Gigha |
| MACGUIRE | Ayrshire, from *MACQUARRIE* |
| MACGURK | Lennox, *MACFARLANE* |
| MACHAFFIE | From MACGUFFIE |
| MACHALE | From *MACDOUGALL* |
| MACHARDY | Deeside; *FARQUHARSON* |
| MACHARDIE | Donside; Clan *CHATTAN*; *MACINTOSH* |
| MACHARG | Galloway 15th c. |
| MACHAROLD | *MACLEOD* of Harris |
| MACHAY | Dumfriesshire 14th c.; *SHAW* |
| MACKHENDRIE, MACHENDRY, MACHENRY | N. Argyll; *MACDONALD* of Glencoe Bute, S. Argyll; *MACNAUGHTON* |
| MACHOWELL | From *MACDOUGALL* |
| MACHRAY | Aberdeenshire, from *MACRAE* |
| MACHUGH, MACHUTCHEN, MACHUTCHEON | *MACDONALD* |
| MACIAN | *MACDONALD* of Ardnamurchan *MACDONALD* of Glencoe Caithness, *GUNN* also *MACGREGOR* |
| MACILDOWIE | Duart *MACLEAN*; *CAMERON* *LAMONT*; *MACGREGOR* |
| MACILDUFF | Dumfries 15th c.; MACILDUY |
| MACILDUY | *MACGREGOR*; *MACLEAN* |
| MACILLRICK | Ayrshire, MACILRIACH |
| MACILREACH | See MACILRIACH |
| MACILREVIE | Islay, Galloway, MACILRIACH |
| MACILRIACH | N. Skye, S.W. Scotland, *MACDONALD* Moray, N.E. Scotland, *FRASER* |
| MACILROY | *GRANT* of Glenmoriston Dumfriesshire 14th c.; *MACGILLIVRAY* |

| SURNAME | CLAN OR DISTRICT SOURCE |
|---------|------------------------|
| MACILVAIN, MACILVEEN | Galloway 14th c.; *MACBEAN* |
| MACILVORA | *MACGILLIVRAY*; *MACLEAN* |
| MACILVRAE | *MACGILLIVRAY* |
| MACILVRIDE | Perthshire 15th c.; *MACDONALD* |
| MACILWHOM | From 'MacIlquham', *LAMONT* |
| MACILWRAITH, MACILWRICK | S.W. Scotland, from MACILRIACH |
| MACIMMEY | From MACSIMON, *FRASER* |
| MACINALLY | *MACFARLANE*; *BUCHANAN* |
| MACINDEOR | Argyll, *BUCHANAN*; Islay, *MACARTHUR*; *MENZIES* |
| MACINDOE | *BUCHANAN* |
| MACINNES | Clan *MACINNES* |
|  | Perthshire, *MACGREGOR* |
| MACINNON | Skye, *MACKINNON* |
| MACINROY | *ROBERTSON* |
| MACINSTALKER | *MACFARLANE*; *MACGREGOR* |
| MACINTOSH | Clan *MACINTOSH*; Clan *CHATTAN* |
| MACINTYRE | Clan *MACINTYRE* |
| MACISAAC | *MACDONALD* of Clanranald |
|  | *CAMPBELL* of Argyll |
| MACIVER, MACIVOR | Argyll, *CAMPBELL* |
|  | Ross and Lewis, *MACKENZIE* |
|  | Perthshire, *ROBERTSON* |
| MACJAMES | *GUNN*; *MACFARLANE*; *ROBERTSON* |
| MACK | Berwickshire 15th c.; *HOME* |
| MACKAIL | From MACCALL, *MACAULAY* |
|  | From MACPHAIL, *CAMERON* |
| MACKAIN, MACKANE | *MACDONALD* of Ardnamurchan |
| MACKAMES | 'MacJames', *GUNN* |
| MACKASKILL | Skye, *MACLEOD* of Lewis |
| MACKAY | Clan *MACKAY* |
|  | Argyll, Galloway, to *MACDONALD* |
| MACKAY | Inverness-shire, *DAVIDSON* |
| MACKEACHAN | From MACEACHAN |
| MACKEACHIE | *MACDONALD* |
| MACKEAMISH | 'MacJames', *GUNN* |
| MACKEAN, MACKEAND | From MACIAN |
| MACKECHNIE | See MACEACHAN |
| MACKEDDIE | From MACADIE |
| MACKEE | Bute, Wigtown 16th c.; from *MACKAY* |
| MACKEGGIE | See EGGIE; *MACINTOSH* |
| MACKEITH | Perthshire, Argyll; *MACPHERSON* |
| MACKEITHAN | From MACCUITHEIN, Skye 17th c. |
| MACKELL | From MACKAIL |
| MACKELLAIG | From MACKELLOCH |
| MACKELLAR | *CAMPBELL* of Argyll |
| MACKELLY, MACKELLOCH | Galloway 12th c., Perthshire etc. 14th c.; *MACDONALD* |
| MACKELVIE | Galloway 13th c.; *CAMPBELL* |
| MACKENDRICK | MACHENRY; *MACNAUGHTON* |
| MACKENNA, MACKENNEY | Wigtownshire 15th c., Bute 17th c.; from *MACKENZIE* |
| MACKENZIE | Clan *MACKENZIE* |
| MACKEOCHAN | See MACEACHAN |

B

| SURNAME | CLAN OR DISTRICT SOURCE |
|---|---|
| MACKEON, MACKEOWN | See MACCUNE |
| MACKERCHAR | See MACERCHAR |
| MACKERLICH, MACKERLIE | Carrick 13th c.; Argyll, *CAMPBELL*; Ross, *MACKENZIE* |
| MACKERRACHER | From MACERRACHER |
| MACKERRAS | Kintyre 16th c.; from MACFERGUS |
| MACKERRELL | Ayrshire 13th c., Galloway 14th c. |
| MACKERRON, MACKIARRAN | S.W. Scotland 12th c.; *MACDONALD* Bute, STUART; Moray, *GRANT* |
| MACKERSEY | From MACKERRAS |
| MACKESSACK, MACKESSICK | From MACISAAC; Moray 16th c.; *CAMPBELL* of Argyll |
| MACKESTER | Kenmore 17th c.; *HAY* |
| MACKEWAN, MACKEWN | See MACCUNE |
| MACKEY | See MACKEE |
| MACKICHAN | *MACDONALD* of Clanranald *MACDOUGALL* |
| MACKIE (Mackie) (McKie) | Stirlingshire 16th c.; *MACKAY* See MACKEE |
| MACKIESON | Moray 14th c.; *MACINTOSH* |
| MACKIGGAN | N. Uist 16th c.; *MACDONALD* |
| MACKILL | Galloway 15th c. |
| MACKILLICAN | *MACINTOSH* |
| MACKILLOP | *MACDONALD* of Glencoe *MACDONALD* of Keppoch |
| MACKIM, MACKIMMIE | From MACSIMON; *FRASER* |
| MACKINDLAY, MACKINLAY, MACKINLEY | Perthshire etc., *MACFARLANE, BUCHANAN*; West coast, from MACDONLEAVY; Deeside, *FARQUHARSON* |
| MACKINNELL | Dumfriesshire, *MACDONALD* |
| MACKINNEY | From MACKENNA |
| MACKINNING | From *MACKINNON* |
| MACKINNON | Clan *MACKINNON*; Clan *ALPIN* |
| MACKINSTRY | Galloway 16th c. |
| MACKINTOSH | From *MACINTOSH* |
| MACKINTYRE | From *MACINTYRE* |
| MACKINVEN | Kintyre 17th c.; *MACKINNON* |
| MACKIRDY | Bute 16th c.; *STUART* |
| MACKISSOCK | See MACKESSACK |
| MACKIVER | Renfrew, from MACIVER |
| MACKNIGHT | Galloway 16th c., from MACNAUGHT |
| MACKUEN, MACKUNE | See MACCUNE |
| MACLACHLAN | Clan *MACLACHLAN* |
| MACLAE | See MACLEAY |
| MACLAGAN | *ROBERTSON* |
| MACLAGHLAN | *MACLACHLAN* |
| MACLAINE | Clan *MACLAINE* of Lochbuie |
| MACLAIRISH | *MACDONALD* |
| MACLAMOND | *LAMONT* |
| MACLARDY | From MACLAVERTY |
| MACLAREN | Clan *MACLAREN* |
| MACLARTY | From MACLAVERTY |

| SURNAME | CLAN OR DISTRICT SOURCE |
|---|---|
| MACLATCHIE | Ayrshire 16th c. |
| MACLAUCHLAN, MACLAUGHLIN | Clan *MACLACHLAN* |
| MACLAURIN | Same as *MACLAREN* |
| MACLAVERTY | Galloway 14th c.; *MACDONALD* |
| MACLAWS | From MACLEHOSE |
| MACLAY, MACLEA | See MACLEAY |
| MACLEAN | Clan *MACLEAN* |
| MACLEAR, MACLEARY | From MACCHLERY |
| MACLEAY | Ross 15th c.; Appin *STEWART* |
| MACLEES, MACLEESH | Same as MACLEISH |
| MACLEHOSE | *CAMPBELL*; Perthshire, *MACTHOMAS* |
| MACLEISH | Dumfriesshire 14th c.; from MACGILLIES |
| MACLEISTER | Argyll etc., *MACGREGOR* |
| MACLELLAN, MACLELLAND | 'MacGilfillan', Galloway 13th c., Inverness 15th c., Perthshire, *MACNAB* |
| MACLEMON | *LAMONT* |
| MACLENNAN | Clan *MACLENNAN* |
| MACLEOD | *MACLEOD* of Harris |
| | *MACLEOD* of Lewis |
| MACLERGAIN | Islay, *MACLEAN* |
| MACLERIE | From MACCHLERY |
| MACLETCHIE | Ayrshire 13th c. |
| MACLEVERTY | See MACLAVERTY |
| MACLEW | Same as MACLEAY |
| MACLEWIS | From MACLOUIS: also *MACLEOD* |
| MACLINDEN | From MACLINTOCK |
| MACLINTOCK | *COLQUHOUN*; Lorne, *MACDOUGALL* |
| MACLISE, MACLISH | See MACLEISH, *MACPHERSON* |
| MACLIVER | *MACGREGOR*; Islay, *CAMPBELL* |
| MACLORG, MACLURG | Ayrshire 13th c. |
| MACLOUIS, MACLOY | Arran, FULLARTON; *STUART* |
| MACLUCAS MACLUCKIE MACLUGASH MACLUKE | Cowal, *LAMONT* N. Argyll, *MACDOUGALL* |
| MACLULLICH | *MACDOUGALL*; *ROSS*; *MUNRO* |
| MACLUNG | Galloway 17th c. |
| MACLURE | Galloway 16th c.; Harris *MACLEOD* |
| MACLYMONT | Carrick 17th c.; *LAMONT* |
| MACMAHON | *MATHESON* |
| MACMAINS, MACMANUS | From 'MacMagnus', COLQUHOUN; GUNN |
| MACMARTIN | Galloway 12th c.; *CAMERON* |
| MACMASTER | *MACINNES*; *BUCHANAN* |
| MACMATH | *MATHESON*; Dumfries, MACNAUGHT |
| MACMAURICE | *BUCHANAN* |
| MACMEEKEN, MACMEIKAN | See MACMICHAN |
| MACMENZIES | Dumfriesshire etc. 14th c.; *MENZIES* |
| MACMICHAEL | Appin and Galloway *STEWART* Aberdeenshire, see MACMICHIE |
| MACMICHAN | Carrick and Galloway 12th c. |
| MACMICHIE | *MACDONELL* of Keppoch |
| MACMILLAN | Clan *MACMILLAN* |

| | |
|---|---|
| MACMIN, MACMINN | Galloway 15th c.; *MENZIES* |
| MACMONIES | Dumfries 16th c.; *MENZIES* |
| MACMORINE | Galloway, MACMORRAN |
| MACMORRAN | Galloway 14th c.; Mull, *MACKINNON* |
| MACMUNN | *LAMONT*, to Bute *STUART* |
| MACMURCHIE | N. Uist, Kintyre, *MACDONALD* |
| MACMURCHY | *BUCHANAN*; *MACKENZIE* |
| MACMURDO, | Kintyre to Dumfriesshire 16th c. |
| MACMURDOCH | *MACDONALD*; *MACPHERSON* |
| MACMURRAY | Galloway, from MACVURICH |
| MACMURRICH | From MACVURICH |
| MACMURTRIE | Ayrshire etc., from MACKIRDY |
| MACNAB, MACNABB | *MACNAB*; Clan *ALPIN* |
| MACNACHTAN, | Same as *MACNAUGHTON* |
| MACNAUGHTEN | |
| MACNAIR | Argyll, *MACNAUGHTON*; Lennox, |
| | *MACFARLANE*; Perthshire, *MACNAB* |
| MACNAIRN | Dumfriesshire 14th c.; Appin *STEWART* |
| MACNAMELL | From '*MACMILLAN*', to *MACDOUGALL* |
| MACNAUCHTON | Same as *MACNAUGHTON* |
| MACNAUGHT | Dumfriesshire 13th c.; *MACNAUGHTON* |
| MACNAUGHTAN, | Clan *MACNAUGHTON* |
| MACNAUGHTON | |
| MACNAY | Same as MACNEE |
| MACNAYER | Same as MACNAIR |
| MACNEAL, MACNEALE | *MACNEIL* |
| MACNEE, MACNEA | *MACGREGOR* |
| MACNEICE | Same as MACNEISH |
| MACNEIL ⎫ | Clan *MACNEIL* of Barra |
| MACNEILL ⎭ | Clan *MACNEILL* of Gigha |
| MACNEILAGE | Lennox 15th c.; *MACNEIL* |
| MACNEISH | *MACINNES*; Dumfriesshire 14th c.; |
| | Strathearn, *MACGREGOR* |
| MACNELLY | Galloway 13th c.; *MACNEIL* |
| MACNESS | Same as MACNEISH |
| MACNEUR | Same as MACNUIR |
| MACNEVIN | Same as MACNIVEN |
| MACNEY | *MACGREGOR* |
| MACNICOL | Sutherland and Skye, MACLEOD of Lewis; |
| MACNICOLL | Glenorchy, *MACFIE* to *CAMPBELL* |
| MACNICHOL | |
| MACNIDER | Ayrshire 15th c.; *MACFARLANE* |
| MACNIE | *MACGREGOR* |
| MACNIEL | Same as *MACNEIL* |
| MACNEISH, MACNISH | See MACNEISH |
| MACNIFF | Kirkcudbrightshire 17th c. |
| MACNITER | See MACNIDER |
| MACNIVEN | Argyll, *MACNAUGHTON*, to *CAMPBELL* |
| | Spey, *MACINTOSH*; *CUMMING* |
| MACNOCAIRD | *MACGREGOR*; *CAMPBELL* |
| MACNUCATOR | *MACGREGOR*; Appin *STEWART* |
| MACNUIR, MACNUYER | Cowal: *MACNAUGHTON*, *BUCHANAN* |
| | Lennox: *MACFARLANE* |
| MACOMIE | From *MACTHOMAS*, *MACINTOSH* |
| MACOMISH | *MACTHOMAS*; *GUNN* |
| MACONACHIE | See MACCONOCHIE |

| | |
|---|---|
| MACONIE | *CAMERON* |
| MACORAN | *CAMPBELL* of Argyll |
| MACO'SHANNAIG | Kintyre 16th c.; *MACDONALD* |
| MACOSTRICH | From 'Macostric'; *CAMERON* |
| MACOUAL, MACOUL | From *MACDOUGALL* |
| MACOUAT, MACOWAT | From MACWATT, *FORBES* |
| MACOWAN, MACOWEN | See MACCOWAN |
| MACPARLAND, MACPARLANE | From *MACFARLANE* |
| MACPATRICK | *LAMONT*; *MACLAREN* |
| MACPETER | Ayrshire 17th c.; *MACGREGOR* |
| MACPETRIE | *MACLAREN*; *MACGREGOR* |
| MACPHADDEN | From MACFADYEN, *MACLEAN* |
| MACPHAIL | *CAMERON*; Clan *CHATTAN* *MACINTOSH*; *MACKAY* |
| MACPHAIT | *MACLAREN* |
| MACPHATER | Argyll, *MACLAREN* |
| MACPHEDRAN ⎱ MACPHEDRON ⎰ | Loch Fyne, *MACAULAY* Lochawe branch, to *CAMPBELL* |
| MACPHEE | Same as *MACFIE* |
| MACPHIEDRAN | Same as MACPHEDRAN |
| MACPHERSON | Clan *MACPHERSON*; Clan *CHATTAN* |
| MACPHIE | Same as *MACFIE* |
| MACPHILIP | Same as *MACKILLOP* |
| MACPHUN | MACMUNN to *MACARTHUR* |
| MACQUAIRE | *MACQUARRIE* |
| MACQUAKER | Galloway 17th c., from MACVICAR |
| MACQUARIE, MACQUARRIE | *MACQUARRIE*, Clan *ALPIN* |
| MACQUAT | Dumfries 16th c., from MACWATT |
| MACQUATTIE | From MACWATTIE |
| MACQUE, MACQUEY | Galloway 17th c., from *MACKAY* |
| MACQUEEN | Clan *MACQUEEN*; Clan *CHATTAN* |
| MACQUEENIE | Galloway 16th c., from *MACKENZIE* |
| MACQUHIRR | Galloway 16th c., from *MACQUARRIE* |
| MACQUIKCAN | Kintyre 16th c.; *MACDONALD* |
| MACQUIRE | From *MACQUARRIE* |
| MACQUISTAN, MACQUISTEN | Same as MACHUTCHEN |
| MACQUOID | *MACKAY* |
| MACRA, MACRACH | Ayrshire etc. 17th c.; *MACRAE* |
| MACRAE | Clan *MACRAE* |
| MACRAILD | *MACLEOD* of Harris |
| MACRAITH | From *MACRAE*; *MACDONALD* |
| MACRANKIN | Ayrshire 16th c.; Coll, *MACLEAN* |
| MACRATH | From *MACRAE* |
| MACRAW, MACRAY | From *MACRAE* |
| MACREARIE | Dumfriesshire 15th c.; *MACDONALD* |
| MACRIE | See MACRA |
| MACRIMMON | Skye, *MACLEOD* of Harris |
| MACRITCHIE | Glenshee, *MACINTOSH* |
| MACROB, MACROBB | Perthshire, *MACFARLANE*; *INNES* *STEWART* of Appin; *GUNN* |
| MACROBBIE | *ROBERTSON*; *DRUMMOND* |
| MACROBERT, MACROBERTS | *ROBERTSON* |

| | |
|---|---|
| MACROBIE | Same as MACROBBIE |
| MACRONALD | *MACDONELL* of Keppoch |
| MACRORIE, MACRORY, MACRURY | *MACDONALD*; *MACLAREN* |
| MACRUER | MACGREWAR, *MACDONALD* |
| MACRYRIE | *MACDONALD* |
| MACSHERRIE | Skye, Mull, *MACKINNON* |
| MACSIMON | *FRASER: MACARTHUR* |
| MACSORLEY | *LAMONT*, to (Islay) *MACDONALD*, and to *CAMERON* |
| MACSPORRAN | Argyll 12th c.; *MACDONALD* (also recognised in the 1970s by Lord Lyon as a clan in its own right) |
| MACSTEVEN | Ayrshire 16th c. |
| MACSWAIN | *MACQUEEN* |
| MACSWAN, MACSWEEN | *MACQUEEN*; *MACDONALD* |
| MACSYMON | See MACSIMON |
| MACTAGGART | Dumfries 15th c. etc.; *ROSS* |
| MACTAUSE | From MACTAVISH |
| MACTAVISH | *CAMPBELL*; Strathglass, *FRASER* Perthshire, see *MACTHOMAS* |
| MACTEAR | See MACTIER |
| MACTHOMAS | Perthshire, Angus 14th c., Clan *MACTHOMAS*; *MACINTOSH*; Clan *CHATTAN* |
| MACTIER, MACTIRE | *ROSS*; Ayrshire, Galloway 16th c.; from *MACINTYRE* |
| MACTURK | Wigtownshire 16th c. |
| MACULRIG | *CAMERON* |
| MACURE | From MACIVER |
| MACVAIL | From MACPHAIL |
| MACVAIN, MACVANE | *MACKENZIE* |
| MACVANISH | From MACBAIN |
| MACVARISH | *MACDONALD* of Clanranald |
| MACVAY, MACVEAGH | *MACLEAN* of Duart |
| MACVEAN | Same as *MACBEAN* |
| MACVEE | From *MACFIE* |
| MACVEY | *MACLEAN* of Duart |
| MACVICAR | *MACNAUGHTON*, to *CAMPBELL* |
| MACVIE | From *MACFIE* |
| MACVINISH | *MACKENZIE* |
| MACVINNIE | From MACWHINNIE |
| MACVITTIE | Galloway 16th c. |
| MACVURIE | *MACDONALD* of Clanranald |
| MACVURICH, MACVURRICH | Argyll, Arran, *MACDONALD* of Clanranald; Perthshire, *MACPHERSON* |
| MACWALRICK | *KENNEDY*, to *CAMERON* |
| MACWALTER | Ayrshire 16th c.; *MACFARLANE* |
| MACWATT | Bute etc. 15th c.; *FORBES* |
| MACWATTIE | *BUCHANAN*; *FORBES* |
| MACWEENY | See MACWHINNIE |
| MACWHAN | *MACDONALD*; *MACQUEEN* |
| MACWHANNELL | Ayr, Perth 16th c.; *MACDONALD* |
| MACWHINNIE | Galloway 16th c.; from *MACKENZIE* |
| MACWHIRR | Dumfries 16th c.; *MACQUARRIE* |
| MACWHIRTER | From MACCHRUITER |

| | |
|---|---|
| MACWILLIAM | *MACLEOD* of Harris; *GUNN* *MACFARLANE*; *ROBERTSON* also *MACGREGOR* |
| MAGREW | *MACGREGOR* |
| MAIN, MAGNUS | Moray, Nairn, etc., *GUNN* From 'Mayne', Perthshire 16th c. |
| MAINLAND | Orkney, Shetland 16th c. |
| MAIR, MAJOR | Perthshire etc. 13th c. |
| MAITLAND | Lauderdale 12th c. |
| MALCOLM, MALCOM | Clan *MALCOLM* |
| MALCOLMSON | Berwickshire 13th c.; *MACLEOD* |
| MALLACE | Perth (Malles) to Angus 15th c. |
| MALLISON | Aberdeen, Dundee 15th c. |
| MALLOCH | Perth, Angus 15th c.; *MACGREGOR* |
| MALLOY | See MILLOY |
| MALTMAN | Aberdeenshire 16th c. |
| MANDERSON | Merse (Manderston) 15th c. |
| MANN, MANSON | 'Magnus-son', *GUNN* |
| MANUEL | Stirlingshire (Manuel) 13th c. |
| MARCHBANKS | From MARJORIBANKS |
| MARGACH | Moray 17th c. |
| MARJORIBANKS | Renfrewshire 16th c.; *JOHNSTON* |
| MARK | Roxburghshire 16th c.; *MACDONALD* |
| MARQUIS | From MacMarquis; *MACDONALD* |
| MARR | Fife, Aberdeenshire 13th c.; *GORDON* |
| MARSHALL | Lothian etc. 12th c.; *KEITH* |
| MARTIN | *CAMERON*; *MACDONALD* |
| MARTIN, MARTINE | E. Lothian, Angus 12th c. |
| MARWICK | Orkney (W. Mainland) 17th c. |
| MASON, MASSON | Berwick, Midlothian etc. 14th c. |
| MASSEY, MASSIE | Aberdeenshire 17th c.; *MATHESON* |
| MASTERS | Same as MACMASTER |
| MASTERSON, MASTERTON | Fife (Dunfermline) 13th c. |
| MATHER, MATHERS | Fife 13th c., Angus 15th c. |
| MATHESON | Clan *MATHESON* Angus etc. 14th c.; and from MACMATH |
| MATHEWSON | See *MATHESON* |
| MATHIE | Angus 15th c.; *MATHESON* |
| MATHIESON | See *MATHESON* |
| MATSON, MATTHEW | See *MATHESON* |
| MAUCHLEN | Ayrshire (Mauchline) 15th c. |
| MAULE | Midlothian 12th c., Angus etc. 13th c. |
| MAVER, MAVOR | Speymouth 15th c.; *GORDON* |
| MAXTON | Dryburgh 13th c., to Perthshire 14th c. |
| MAXWELL | Clan *MAXWELL* |
| MAY | Berwick 13th c., Fife 14th c.; and OMAY |
| MEANIE, MEANEY | Aberdeenshire (Meanie) 17th c. |
| MEANIES, MEANS | From *MENZIES* |
| MECHIE, MEKIE | From MICHIE |
| MEECHAN, MEEHAN | From MACMICHAN |
| MEEK, MEIK | Fife, Angus 15th c., Perthshire 16th c. |
| MEEKISON | From MACMICHIE |
| MEFFAN, MEFFET | See METHVEN; *MOFFAT* |
| MEIKLE | Aberdeenshire, Moray 14th c. |
| MEIKLEHAM | From 'MacIlquham', *LAMONT* |

| | |
| --- | --- |
| MEIKLEJOHN | Fife etc. 17th c. |
| MEIKLEM | See MEIKLEHAM |
| MEIN, MEINE | Roxburgh 14th c.; and from *MENZIES* |
| MELDRUM | *FORBES*; *GORDON* |
| MELLIS, MELLISH | Aberdeenshire 15th c. ('Malise') |
| MELLON, MELLEN | Moray Firth, from MELVIN |
| MELROSE | Roxburghshire 15th c. |
| MELVILLE | Midlothian, Angus 12th c. |
| MELVIN, MELVEN | Angus etc. 14th c., from MELVILLE |
| MENELAWS | E. Ross and Lauder 15th c. |
| MENGUES | From *MENZIES* |
| MENTEITH | *GRAHAM*; *STEWART* |
| MENTIPLAY | Caithness 17th c., from MONEYPENNY |
| MENZIES | Clan *MENZIES* |
| MERCER | Tillicoultry, Perth etc. 13th c. |
| MERCHANT | Fife and Angus 13th c. |
| MERRILEES | W. Lothian 16th c. |
| MESSENGER | Midlothian, Dumfries 17th c. |
| MESSER | Stirlingshire 15th c., Aberdeen etc. 17th c. |
| METHVEN, METHUEN | Perthshire (Methven) 13th c. |
| MICHAEL | Angus 15th c.; Keppoch *MACDONNELL* |
| MICHIE | Keppoch *MACDONNELL*, to *FORBES* |
| MICHIESON | From MACMICHIE |
| MICKEL, MICKLE | Same as MEIKLE |
| MIDDLEMASS, MIDDLEMIST, etc. | Kelso, to Peeblesshire 15th c. |
| MIDDLETON | Laurencekirk 13th c.; *FORBES* |
| MILES | Melrose etc. 16th c. |
| MILL | Angus, Aberdeen 15th c.; *GORDON* |
| MILLAR, MILLER | Moray 14th c., Glasgow etc. 15th c.; *MACFARLANE* |
| MILLIGAN | Galloway 13th c., Perth 15th c. |
| MILLIKEN | Same as MILLIGAN |
| MILLOY | From MACLOY, *STUART* of Bute |
| MILLS, MILN, MILNE, MILNES | Aberdeenshire 14th c.; *GORDON* |
| MILROY | From MACILROY, *MACGILLIVRAY* |
| MINN, MINNUS | Galloway, from *MENZIES* |
| MINTO | Teviotdale (Minto) 17th c. |
| MIRK | Glasgow 15th c., Kelso etc. 16th c. |
| MITCHELHILL | Peeblesshire, to Selkirk 16th c. |
| MITCHELL | From MACMICHAEL; Lanarkshire 15th c. |
| MITCHELSON | Fife 14th c., and MACMICHAEL |
| MOAR | Orkney 15th c. |
| MOCHRIE | S.E. Stirlingshire 17th c. |
| MOFFAT, MOFFETT | Annandale 13th c. (now recognised as a clan in its own right) |
| MOIR | Aberdeenshire 14th c.; *GORDON* |
| MOLLISON | Aberdeen 16th c.; from MALLISON |
| MONACH | Perthshire, *MACFARLANE* |
| MONCRIEFF | Strathearn, to Angus 13th c. |
| MONCUR | Fife 13th c., Angus 14th c. |
| MONRO, MONROE | Same as *MUNRO* |
| MONTEATH, MONTEITH | Same as MENTEITH |
| MONTGOMERIE, MONTGOMERY | Renfrewshire 12th c. |

| SURNAME | CLAN OR DISTRICT SOURCE |
|---|---|
| MONYPENNY | Fife 13th c., Stirlingshire 15th c. |
| MOODIE, MOODY | Tweed 13th c., Angus 15th c.; *STEWART* |
| MOORE | Same as MUIR |
| MORAY | Same as *MURRAY* |
| MORE | From MOIR, also MUIR; *LESLIE* |
| MORGAN | Aberdeenshire etc. 13th c.; *MACKAY* |
| MORHAM, MORAM | E. Lothian 12th c., Angus etc. 13th c. |
| MORISON | Clan *MORRISON*; Perthshire, *BUCHANAN* |
| MORREN, MORRIN | Dumfries etc., from MACMORRAN |
| MORRIS, MORRICE | Ayrshire, Aberdeen etc. 16th c.; *GORDON*; Perthshire, *BUCHANAN* |
| MORRISON | Clan *MORRISON*; Perthshire, *BUCHANAN* |
| MORTIMER | Fife etc. 12th c. |
| MORTON | Nithsdale 12th c., Fife 14th c.; *DOUGLAS* |
| MOSS | Nithsdale 14th c., Tweed 16th c. |
| MOSSMAN | Tweed 15th c., Edinburgh etc. 16th c. |
| MOUAT, MOWATT | Angus 12th c., Cromarty 13th c.; *SUTHERLAND* |
| MOULTRIE | Berwick 13th c., Edinburgh 14th c. |
| MOUNSEY, MOUNSIE | Roxburghshire 13th c., Lochmaben 14th c. |
| MOWBRAY | Fife, Lothian 12th c. |
| MOYES | Angus 13th c., Lanarkshire 15th c. |
| MUCKHART | Clackmannanshire 13th c., Aberdeen 16th c. |
| MUDIE | See MOODIE |
| MUIL, MUILL | Nairn 13th c., Aberdeen etc. 17th c. |
| MUIR, MURE | Galloway, Ayrshire 13th c.; *GORDON* |
| MUIRHEAD | Roxburghshire 14th c., Lanarkshire 15th c. |
| MUNDELL, MUNDLE | Dumfriesshire, Wigtownshire 13th c. |
| MUNGALL, MUNGLE | Falkirk, to Ayrshire etc. 13th c. |
| MUNN | From MACMUNN |
| MUNNOCH, MUNNOCK | Fife etc., from MONACH |
| MUNRO, MUNROE | Clan *MUNRO* |
| MUNSIE | See MOUNSIE |
| MURCHIE, MURCHISON | From MACMURCHIE |
| MURDOCH, MURDOCK | From MACMURCHIE, also MACMURDOCH |
| MURDOSON | *MACDONALD*; *MACPHERSON* |
| MURIE | Gowrie (Murie) 17th c. |
| MURISON | Fife, Angus, Aberdeenshire 15th c. |
| MURPHY | Arran, Kintyre, *MACDONALD* |
| MURRAY | *MURRAY*; *SUTHERLAND* |
| MURRIE | Perthshire, *MURRAY* |
| MUSHET | Angus etc. 12th c.; *DRUMMOND* |
| MUSTARD | Angus etc. 16th c. |
| MUTCH | Stirlingshire 16th c. |
| MUTRIE | From MOULTRIE |
| MYLES | See MILES |
| MYLNE | See MILNE |
| NAIRN, NAIRNE | Nairn etc. 14th c.; *MACINTOSH* |
| NAISMITH | Angus 15th c., Lanarkshire etc. 16th c. |
| NAPIER, NAPPER | Lennox 13th c.; *MACFARLANE*; *SCOTT* |
| NASMYTH, NAYSMITH | See NAISMITH |
| NEAL, NEALE | *MACNEIL* |
| NEAVES | From BALNEAVES, *MURRAY* |
| NEIL, NEILL | *MACNEIL* |
| NEILLANDS | From NEWLANDS |

| | |
| --- | --- |
| NEILSON | *MACKAY*, and to *GUNN* |
| | Ayrshire 13th c.; *STUART* of Bute |
| | From *MACNEIL* |
| NEISH | From MACNEISH, *MACGREGOR* |
| NELSON | Same as NEILSON; *MACGREGOR* |
| NESBET, NESBITT | Same as NISBET |
| NESS | Fife and Renfrewshire 12th c. |
| NEVILLE | Perth 13th c. |
| NEVIN, NEVISON | See NIVEN, NIVISON |
| NEWBIGGING | Lanarkshire 13th c., etc. |
| NEWLANDS | Dumfriesshire, W. Lothian 15th c. |
| NEWTON | Midlothian 13th c., etc. |
| NICE | See NISH |
| NICOL, NICHOL | Roxburghshire, Angus 12th c.; also |
| NICOLL, NICHOLL | from MACNICOL |
| NICHOLS, NICOLS | From NICHOLAS; Glasgow, Aberdeen etc. |
| NICOLSON | 15th c. From MACNICOL, *MACLEOD* |
| NICHOLSON | of Lewis |
| NIEL, NIELSON | See NEIL, NEILSON |
| NIMMO | W. Lothian 15th c., Glasgow 16th c. |
| NISBET, NISBETT | Berwickshire 12th c.; *HOME* |
| NISH, NICE | From MACNEISH; Fife, from NESS |
| NIVEN, NIVISON | Lanarkshire 13th c., Ayrshire 16th c.; and from MACNIVEN |
| NIXON | Liddesdale 14th c.; *ARMSTRONG* |
| NOBLE | E. Lothian 12th c.; *MACINTOSH* |
| NOON | Aberdeen 16th c. |
| NORIE, NORRIE | Orkney etc.; Lewis *MACLEOD* |
| NORMAN, NORMAND | Aberdeen, Tweed (Normanville) 12th c. From 'Tormod'; Harris *MACLEOD* |
| NORRIS | Berwickshire 12th c. |
| NORVAL, NORWELL | From 'Normanville': see NORMAN |
| NOTMAN | E. Lothian 16th c. |
| NUCATOR | Angus 16th c., from MACNUCATOR |
| | |
| OAG, OAKE | Same as OGG |
| OCHILTREE | W. Lothian 14th c.; *CAMPBELL* |
| OFFICER | Kincardineshire etc. 13th c. |
| OGG | Aberdeenshire 15th c. |
| OGILBY | Same as *OGILVIE* |
| OGILVIE, OGILVY | Clan *OGILVIE* |
| OGSTON, OGSTOUN | Elgin 13th c. |
| OLIPHANT | Roxburghshire, OLIVER; *SUTHERLAND* |
| OLIVER | Roxburghshire 12th c.; *FRASER* |
| OLLASON | Shetland 16th c. |
| OMAN, OMAND | Orkney, Shetland 16th c. |
| OMAY, O'MAY | Kintyre 16th c.; *MACDONALD* |
| ORAM, OREM | Aberdeen 15th c. |
| ORKNEY | Angus etc. 15th c. |
| ORMISTON | Roxburghshire, E. Lothian 12th c. |
| ORR | S.W. Renfrewshire 13th c.; *CAMPBELL* of Argyll; *MACGREGOR* |
| ORROCK, ORRICK | Fife (Burntisland) 13th c. |
| OSBORN, OSBORNE | Ayrshire etc. 16th c. |
| OSLER, OSTLERE | Moray 15th c. |

| | |
|---------|-------------------------|
| OSWALD | Ayrshire, Fife, Orkney 17th c. |
| OTTER | Berwick 13th c., Fife 15th c. |
| OVENS | E. Lothian 17th c. |
| | |
| PADON | Same as PATON |
| PAGAN, PAIN | Renfrewshire 13th c. |
| PAGE | Aberdeenshire, Angus 14th c. |
| PAINTER, PANTER | Angus 14th c. |
| PAIRMAN | E. Teviotdale 16th c. |
| PAISLEY | Renfrewshire 12th c. |
| PALMER | Tweedside, Glasgow etc. 13th c. |
| PANTON | Lanarkshire 13th c., Aberdeenshire 15th c. |
| PAPE | Same as POPE |
| PAPLAY | Orkney 14th c. |
| PARIS | Ayrshire etc. 13th c. |
| PARK, PARKE | Renfrew (Erskine), to Berwickshire 13th c.; S. Uist, *MACDONALD* of Clanranald |
| PARKER | Perthshire 13th c., Dundee 14th c. |
| PARLAN, PARLANE | From *MACFARLANE* |
| PATE | Fife 16th c., Lanarkshire 17th c. |
| PATERSON | From MACPHEDRAN: also MACPATRICK |
| PATTERSON | Aberdeenshire, *FARQUHARSON* |
| PATON | *MACDONALD*; Lochbuie *MACLAINE* |
| PATRICK | Ayrshire 15th c.; and from MACPATRICK |
| PATTEN, PATTON } | See PATON |
| PATTIE, PATTISON } | Fife 16th c., Paisley etc. 16th c. |
| PATTINSON | Edinburgh, Aberdeen 15th c., Dumfries 16th c. |
| PATTULLO | Fife, Perth 14th c.; *MACGREGOR* |
| PAUL | See MACPHAIL |
| PAULIN, PAULINE | W. Lothian, Angus 14th c. |
| PAXTON | E. Berwickshire (Paxton) 13th c. |
| PEACE | Orkney 15th c. |
| PEACOCK | Dumfriesshire 13th c. |
| PEARSON | Berwickshire 15th c.; *MACPHERSON* |
| PEAT | Aberdeen 15th c., from PETER |
| PEATTIE, PEDDIE | Fife and Angus 15th c. |
| PEDEN | Ayrshire 17th c., from PATON |
| PEEBLES | Tweeddale, also Angus 14th c. |
| PENDER | Lanarkshire 16th c. |
| PENDREICH | Stirlingshire, PITTENDREIGH |
| PENMAN | Tweedside 17th c. |
| PENNEY, PENNY | Moray and Perthshire 14th c. |
| PENNYCOOK, etc. | Midlothian (Penicuik) 13th c. |
| PENTLAND | Midlothian 13th c. |
| PERRY | Angus 15th c., Aberdeen 17th c. |
| PETER | Aberdeen 14th c.; *MACGREGOR* |
| PETERKIN | Aberdeen 15th c.; *MACGREGOR* |
| PETERS, PETERSON | *MACLAREN*; *MACGREGOR* |
| PETRIE | *MACLAREN*; *MACGREGOR* |
| PETTIE, PETTITT | Lanarkshire 13th c., Ayr etc. 14th c. |
| PETTIGREW | Lanarkshire 13th c. |
| PHILP, PHILLIP } | |
| PHILIPSON | Berwick and Lanarkshire 13th c., |
| PHILLIPS | Aberdeen and Fife 15th c.; |
| PHILP, PHILPOT } | also from MACKILLOP |
| PHIMISTER | Moray 15th c. |

| | |
|---|---|
| PHIN | Fife 16th c., Banffshire 16th c. |
| PICKEN | Ayrshire, Edinburgh 17th c. |
| PIGGOT, PIGOTT | Berwickshire, Aberdeenshire 14th c. |
| PILLAN, PILLANS | Lanarkshire (Carstairs) 16th c. |
| PINKERTON | E. Lothian 13th c., to *CAMPBELL* 16th c. |
| PIPER, PYPER | Perthshire 16th c.; *MURRAY* |
| PIRIE, PIRRIE | Aberdeenshire, Renfrewshire 15th c. |
| PITCAIRN | Fife (Pitcairn) 13th c. |
| PITKETHLY, etc. | E. Strathearn (Pitcaithly) 13th c. |
| PITTENDREIGH | Moray 13th c., Wigtown 14th c. etc. |
| PLAYFAIR | Orkney 13th c., Fife 16th c. |
| PLENDERLEITH | Roxburghshire (Oxham) 13th c. |
| PLUMMER, PLUMER | Kelso, to Angus 14th c. |
| POLE, POLESON | Shetland 17th c.; *MACKAY* |
| POLK, POOK | From POLLOCK |
| POLLOCK, POLLOK | Renfrew and Moray 12th c., Angus 13th c. |
| POLSON | Berwickshire 12th c., W. Lothian 16th c. |
| POLLARD | From 'Paulson', *MACKAY* |
| PONT | Perth 13th c., Ayr 14th c., Aberdeen 16th c. |
| PONTON | Ayrshire 14th c. |
| POOL, POOLE | Dundee 14th c., Dumfries etc. 17th c. |
| POPE | Elgin 14th c., to Ross etc. 16th c. |
| PORTEOUS | Peeblesshire 15th c. |
| PORTER | Lanarkshire, Angus etc. 13th c. |
| | Glenlyon; *MACNAUGHTON* |
| POTTER | Dumbarton, Moffat 14th c. etc. |
| POTTINGER | Orkney 16th c. |
| POTTS, POTT | Kelso 16th c., from PHILPOT |
| POW, POWE | Glasgow 16th c., Berwickshire 17th c. |
| POWER | Ayrshire 16th c. |
| POWRIE | Angus (Errol) 14th c. |
| PRATT | Nairn etc. 13th c.; *GRANT* |
| PRESTON | S.E. Edinburgh 13th c. |
| PRETSELL, etc. | Peeblesshire (Pratshill) 16th c. |
| PRIMROSE | W. Fife, to Midlothian 14th c. |
| PRINGLE | Gala Water (Hoppringle) 13th c. |
| PRIOR | Dundee and Perth 16th c. |
| PROCTOR | Angus etc. 15th c. |
| PROUDFOOT | Berwickshire 14th c., Carnwarth etc. 17th c. |
| PROVAN, PROVEN | Glasgow 12th c., Strathblane 13th c. |
| PRYDE | Renfrew 13th c., Fife 16th c. |
| PULLAR, PULLER | Perth 14th c. |
| PUNTON | Haddington 16th c., W. Lothian 17th c. |
| PURCELL, PURSELL | Lanark 15th c.; *MACDONALD* |
| PURDIE | Peeblesshire 14th c., Angus 16th c. |
| PURDOM, PURDON | Liddesdale and Glasgow 15th c. |
| PURVES | Berwickshire 13th c. |
| PYOTT, PYE | Inverness 14th c., Fife 17th c.; *GRAHAM* |
| | |
| QUARRIER | Dunkeld 16th c. |
| QUARRY | *MACQUARRIE* |
| QUINTON, QUENTIN | Kelso 13th c., Edinburgh etc. 17th c. |
| | |
| RAE | Dumfriesshire etc. 13th c.; *MACRAE* |
| RAEBURN | N. Ayrshire (Ryburn) 14th c. |
| RAFFLES | S. Annandale (Raffles) 13th c. |

| | |
| --- | --- |
| RAINNIE, RAINY | 'Ranald', W. Fife 14th c., Angus etc. 15th c., Keppoch *MACDONNELL* |
| RAIT, RAITT | Nairn 13th c., Angus etc. 15th c. |
| RAITH | Ayr (Raith) 15th c.; *MACRAE* |
| RAMAGE | Perth 14th c., Stobo etc. 16th c. |
| RAMSAY | Midlothian (Dalhousie) 12th c. (now a clan in its own right) |
| RANDALL, RANDELL | Fife 13th c., Orkney 14th c. |
| RANDOLPH | Fife, Roxburgh 13th c.; *BRUCE* |
| RANKEILLOR | Cupar-Fife 13th c. |
| RANKEN, RANKIN, RANKINE | Ayrshire 15th c.; *MACLEAN* |
| RATTER | Caithness (Ratter), to Orkney 15th c. |
| RATTRAY | Gowrie 15th c. |
| RAY, REA | See RAE |
| READ, REED | Same as REID |
| READDIE, REDDIE | Angus (Reedie), to Fife 16th c. |
| REAY | *MACRAE*; *MACKAY* |
| REDDEN, REDDIN | Kelso (Redden) 12th c. |
| REDPATH, REIDPATH | Lauderdale (Earlston) 13th c. |
| REE | From MACRIE, *MACRAE* |
| REEKIE | Angus etc. 16th c. |
| REIACH | Fife, from RIACH: *FARQUHARSON* |
| REID, REED | Aberdeenshire, Ayrshire 14th c. Perthshire, *ROBERTSON* |
| REIDFURD | Aberdeenshire etc. 16th c.; *INNES* |
| REITH | From MACRAITH, *MACRAE* |
| RENDALL, RENDLE | Same as RANDALL |
| RENNIE, RENNY | From Ranald, see RAINNIE |
| RENTON | Berwick (Coldingham) 13th c. |
| RENWICK, RENNICK | Lanarkshire etc. 17th c. |
| RETTIE | Banffshire, to Aberdeen 15th c. |
| REVAN, REVANS | *MACQUEEN* |
| REVIE | S.W. Scotland, from MACILRIACH |
| RHIND, RHYND | Perthshire etc. 14th c.; *LINDSAY* |
| RIACH, REOCH | *FARQUHARSON*; *MACDONALD* |
| RICHARDSON | Clyde 14th c.; *OGILVIE*; *BUCHANAN* |
| RIDDELL, RIDDLE | Roxburghshire, Midlothian 12th c. |
| RIDLAND | Orkney (Redland), to Shetland 17th c. |
| RIGG | Ayr, Dumfries etc. 16th c. |
| RINTOUL | Kinross-shire, Perthshire 16th c. |
| RIPLEY | Moray 13th c.; *MACINTOSH* |
| RISK | Stirlingshire 16th c.; *BUCHANAN* |
| RITCHIE | Border 16th c.; *MACINTOSH* |
| ROBB | *MACFARLANE*; Appin *STEWART* |
| ROBBIE | See MACROBBIE |
| ROBERTON | Lanarkshire (Roberton) 13th c. |
| ROBERTS | *ROBERTSON* |
| ROBERTSON | Clan *ROBERTSON* |
| ROBISON, ROBSON | Tweed 15th c.; *GUNN*; *ROBERTSON* |
| ROBINS | *MACGREGOR* |
| ROBINSON | Ayrshire, Glasgow 15th c.; *GUNN* |
| ROCHE, ROCK | Edinburgh 13th c., Aberdeen 15th c. |
| RODERICK | *MACDONALD* |
| RODGER, ROGER | Angus 15th c., Glasgow 16th c. |
| RODGERS, RODGIE | Aberdeen 16th c., Angus etc. 17th c. |

| SURNAME | CLAN OR DISTRICT SOURCE |
|---|---|
| ROGERSON, ROGERS | Aberdeen 13th c., Angus etc. 15th c. |
| ROLLAND | Perthshire, Ayrshire 13th c. |
| ROLLO, ROLLOCK | Perthshire 12th c. (Rollo is now a clan in its own right) |
| ROMANES | Peeblesshire (Rommano) 13th c. |
| ROME | Annandale 16th c.; *JOHNSTON* |
| RONALD, RONALDSON | MACDONNELL of Keppoch |
| RORIE, RORISON | *MACDONALD*; *MACLAREN* |
| ROSE | Clan ROSE |
| ROSIE, ROSEY | N.E. Caithness 17th c. |
| ROSS | Clan *ROSS*; and from *ROSE* |
| ROUGH | Lanarkshire, Linlithgow 15th c. |
| ROUGHHEAD | Berwickshire etc. 15th c. |
| ROUSAY, ROWSAY | Orkney 17th c. |
| ROWAN, ROWAND | From ROLLAND |
| ROWAT, ROWATT | Glasgow 16th c. |
| ROWE, ROW | Dunbartonshire (Rhu) 13th c. |
| ROXBURGH | Roxburghshire etc. 12th c. |
| ROY | From MACINROY; Galloway MILROY; also *MACGREGOR* |
| RULE | Roxburghshire (Rule) 13th c. |
| RUNCIMAN | Roxburghshire 15th c., Moray 16th c. |
| RUSK | Strathearn, *BUCHANAN* |
| RUSKIN | Lorne, *BUCHANAN* |
| RUSSELL, RUSSEL | Tweedside 12th c.; *CUMMING* |
| RUST | Aberdeenshire 16th c. |
| RUTHERFORD | Roxburghshire 12th c. |
| RUTHVEN | Angus and Perthshire 12th c. |
| RYRIE | (MACREARIE) *MACDONALD* |
| | |
| SADDLER, SADLER | Roxburgh 14th c., Ayr, Perth etc. 15th c. |
| SALMON, SALMOND | Perthshire 15th c. |
| SALTON | E. Lothian and Linlithgow 14th c. |
| SAMSON, SAMPSON | Lanarkshire 16th c., Merse 17th c. |
| SANDEMAN | Perthshire (Alyth) 17th c. |
| SANDERS, SANDER | See SAUNDERS |
| SANDERSON | *MACDONELL* of Glengarry |
| SANDILANDS | Upper Clyde 14th c.; *DOUGLAS* |
| SANDISON | Shetland (Sandsound) 15th c.; *GUNN* |
| SANDS | W. Fife (Sands) 15th c. |
| SANGSTER, SANG | Aberdeenshire 15th c. |
| SAUNDERS | Perth 15th c. etc.; *MACDONELL* of Glengarry; *MACALISTER* |
| SAVAGE, SAVIDGE | Edinburgh, Sanquhar 17th c. |
| SCALES | Dumfriesshire, Merse 17th c. |
| SCARLETT | Annandale 13th c., Caithness 14th c. |
| SCARTH | Orkney (Scarth) 15th c. |
| SCLATER | Aberdeen 14th c., Angus etc. 15th c. |
| SCOBIE, SCOBBIE | Perthshire 14th c.; *MACKAY* |
| SCOLLAY | Orkney (Skaill) 16th c. |
| SCORGIE | Aberdeenshire 17th c. |
| SCOTLAND | Kinross-shire 17th c. |
| SCOTT | Clan *SCOTT* |
| SCOUGAL, SCOUGALL | E. Lothian (Scougall) 13th c. |
| SCOULAR, SCOULLER | Berwickshire 16th c. |
| SCRIMGEOUR | Fife and Angus 13th c. (now a clan in its own right) |

| SURNAME | CLAN OR DISTRICT SOURCE |
|---|---|
| SCROGGIE | Perthshire 15th c., Aberdeen 16th c. |
| SEATH | Fife, *SHAW* |
| SEATON | Annandale 12th c., E. Lothian 14th c. |
| SEATTER, SEATER | Orkney (Setter) 16th c. |
| SEGGIE | Kinross-shire (Seggie) 15th c. |
| SELKIRK, SELCRAIG | Selkirk 13th c., to Edinburgh 14th c. |
| SELLAR, SELLARS | Aberdeen 13th c.; from SADDLER |
| SEMPLE, SEMPILL | Renfrewshire 13th c. |
| SERLE | Perth 13th c. |
| SERVICE | Roxburghshire, Stirling 13th c. |
| SETH | Fife, *SHAW* |
| SETON | Same as SEATON |
| SHADE, SHEED | Edinburgh 16th c. |
| SHAND | Aberdeenshire 16th c. |
| SHANK, SHANKS | Midlothian 14th c., Lanarkshire 15th c. |
| SHANNON | Galloway 14th c.; *MACDONALD* |
| SHARP, SHARPE | Peeblesshire 14th c., Perthshire 15th c.; Bute, from MACELHERAN; *STUART* |
| SHAW | Renfrewshire, Lanarkshire 13th c.; *SHAW*; Clan *CHATTAN* |
| SHEACH | Moray etc.; *SHAW* |
| SHEARER, SHERAR | Fife, Aberdeen etc. 14th c. |
| SHEDDEN, SHEDDON | Renfrewshire, Ayrshire 17th c. |
| SHENNAN | Same as SHANNON |
| SHEPHERD | Peebles 13th c., Moray 14th c. etc. |
| SHERET, SHERRATT | Dunbartonshire, Aberdeen 17th c. |
| SHERIFF, SHERIFFS | Aberdeen 14th c. |
| SHERRIE, SHERRY | From MACSHERRIE, *MACKINNON* |
| SHEWAN | Aberdeen 15th c., Shetland etc. 17th c. |
| SHIACH | Moray etc.; *SHAW* |
| SHIELD, SHIELL SHIELS, SHIELDS | Tweeddale and Midlothian 13th c., Glasgow etc. 15th c. |
| SHIERLAW, SHIRLAW | Lanarkshire 15th c. |
| SHILLINGLAW | Peeblesshire (Traquair) 17th c. |
| SHIRRAS, SHIRREFF | See SHERIFF |
| SHIVAS, SHIVES | E. Aberdeenshire (Shivas) 14th c. |
| SHOOLBREAD | Fife (Auchtermuchty) 17th c. |
| SHORT, SHORTT | Stirlingshire 15th c., Dumfries 17th c. |
| SHORTREED | Selkirk, Kelso 17th c. |
| SIBBALD | Fife etc. 13th c. |
| SILVER | Angus, Mearns 15th c. |
| SIM, SIME | Lanarkshire etc. 16th c.; *FRASER* |
| SIMON, SIMONS | Perth 13th c., Aberdeen 15th c.; *FRASER* |
| SIMPSON | From SIMSON |
| SIMSON, SIMS | Edinburgh etc. 15th c.; *FRASER* |
| SINCLAIR | Clan *SINCLAIR* |
| SINTON | E. Selkirkshire (Sinton) 13th c. |
| SIVES | Haddington 17th c., from SHIVAS |
| SIVEWRIGHT | Angus 16th c.; and from CRERAR |
| SKAE, SKEA | Orkney (Skea) 15th c. |
| SKED, SKEDD | E. Midlothian 17th c. |
| SKENE, SKEEN | Clan *SKENE* |
| SKEOCH | Glasgow etc. 16th c. |
| SKIMMING | Galloway, from MACSKIMMING |
| SKINNER | Aberdeen 13th c., Inverness etc. 14th c.; *MACGREGOR* |

| | |
|---|---|
| SLATER, SLATTER | See SCLATER |
| SLEIGH | Aberdeen 13th c. |
| SLESSOR, SLESSER | Aberdeen 15th c. |
| SLIMON, SLIMMAN | Perthshire 15th c., Kelso etc. 16th c. |
| SLOAN, SLOANE | Midlothian, Galloway etc. 16th c. |
| SLORA, SLORACH | Moray etc. 16th c.; *DAVIDSON* |
| SMAIL, SMALE SMALL, SMEALL } | Border 14th c., Aberdeen 15th c.; *MURRAY* |
| SMART, SMAIRT | Fife 14th c., Angus 15th c.; *MACKENZIE* |
| SMEATON | Midlothian (Smeaton) 13th c. |
| SMELLIE, SMILLIE | Lanarkshire 17th c. |
| SMIBERT | Midlothian 15th c., E. Lothian 16th c. |
| SMITH, SMYTHE | S.E. Scotland 13th c.; *MACPHERSON*; *MACFARLANE* |
| SNEDDON, SNEDDAN | S. Mearns (Snadoun); SNOWDEN |
| SNELL | Ayrshire, Glasgow 15th c. |
| SNODGRASS | Ayrshire (Irvine) 14th c. |
| SNOWDEN, SNOWDON | Lauder (Snowden) etc. 17th c. |
| SOMERVILLE | Lanarkshire 12th c., Roxburgh 13th c. |
| SORBIE | Wigtownshire (Sorbie) 13th c. |
| SORLEY, SORLIE | From MACSORLEY |
| SOUNESS | Lauderdale and Aberdeenshire 17th c. |
| SOUTAR, SOUTER | Dumfries 13th c., Perth etc. 14th c. |
| SPALDING | Mearns etc. 13th c.; *MURRAY* |
| SPANKIE | Angus 15th c. |
| SPARK, SPARKE | Aberdeen, Perth 15th c. |
| SPEED | Angus 15th c. |
| SPEEDIE, SPEEDY | Dunfermline etc. 16th c. |
| SPEIRS, SPIERS | Ayrshire 15th c., Stirling 16th c. |
| SPENCE, SPENS | Moray, Ayrshire etc. 13th c.; *MACDUFF* |
| SPINK, SPINKS | Elgin 13th c., Arbroath 17th c. |
| SPITTAL, SPITTEL | Dunbartonshire 14th c.; *BUCHANAN* |
| SPORRAN | *MACDONALD* |
| SPOTTISWOOD | Berwickshire (Gordon) 13th c. |
| SPOWART | Clackmannan, Fife 17th c. |
| SPROTT, SPROAT | Kirkcudbrightshire 13th c. |
| SPROUL, SPREULL | Lennox 13th c.; *MACFARLANE* |
| SPRUNT, SPROUNT | Angus 15th c. |
| SQUAIR, SQUIRE | Midlothian 13th c., Fife 14th c. |
| STABLES, STABLE | Angus 15th c. |
| STALKER | *MACFARLANE*; *MACGREGOR* |
| STANFORD | Glasgow 12th c., Perth 13th c. |
| STANLEY | Edinburgh 15th c., Glasgow 17th c. |
| STARK | Lanarkshire 16th c.; *ROBERTSON* |
| STEEDMAN, STEDMAN | Angus, Fife etc. 16th c. |
| STEEL, STEELE | Border 13th c., Edinburgh etc. 15th c. |
| STEIN, STEEN | 'Steven'; Ayrshire 15th c. etc. |
| STENHOUSE | Falkirk 13th c., Fife 16th c.; *BRUCE* |
| STEPHEN, STEVENS, STEPHENSON | See STEVENSON |
| STEUART | *STEWART* |
| STEVENSON | Ayrshire 12th c., Moray 13th c., Angus 15th c. |
| STEWART | Clan *STEWART* |
| | STEWART of Appin |
| | *STEWART* of Atholl |
| | *STEWART* of Galloway |

| | |
|---|---|
| STILL | Aberdeen 15th c. |
| STILLIE | E. Lothian 13th c., Lanark 17th c. |
| STIRLING | Stirling 12th c., Perthshire etc. 13th c.; also *MACGREGOR* |
| STIRRAT, STIRIE | C. Ayrshire (Stair) 14th c. |
| STOBIE, STOBBIE | Berwick, Perth 14th c. |
| STODDART | Kirkcudbrightshire 14th c. |
| STONE | Roxburghshire 13th c., Aberdeen 15th c. |
| STOREY, STORRIE | Angus, Aberdeen 13th c.; *OGILVIE* |
| STORRAR, STORER | Banffshire etc. 16th c. |
| STOTT, STOUT | Aberdeen 13th c., Tweeddale 17th c. |
| STOVE | Orkney (Sanday), to Shetland 17th c. |
| STRACHAN | Kincardineshire (Strathachen) 11th c. |
| STRANG, STRANGE | Angus 13th c., Aberdeen 14th c. |
| STRATHERN | Strathearn 12th c. |
| STRATHIE | Perthshire 13th c. |
| STRATON, STRATTON | Midlothian 13th c., Aberdeen 15th c. |
| STRINGER | Aberdeen 15th c.; *MACGREGOR* |
| STRONACH | Moray etc. 15th c. |
| STRUTHERS | Roxburghshire etc. 16th c. |
| STUART | *STUART* of Bute; *STEWART* |
| STURROCK | Angus, Aberdeen 15th c. |
| SUMMERS, SUMNER | Perth, Angus 14th c.; *LINDSAY* |
| SUTHERLAND | Clan *SUTHERLAND* |
| SUTTIE | E. Lothian etc. 17th c.; *GRANT* |
| SWAN, SWANN | *MACQUEEN*; *GUNN* |
| SWANSON, SWANNEY | Caithness, Orkney, *GUNN* |
| SWANSTON | Midlothian 13th c., Tweedside 16th c. |
| SWIFT | Edinburgh 15th c. |
| SWINTON | Berwickshire 11th c. |
| SWORD | 'Siward', S.E. Scotland 14th c. |
| SYM, SYME | See SIM |
| SYMINGTON | Upper Clydesdale 14th c. |
| SYMON, SYMONS | See SIMON |
| | |
| TAGGART | Dumfries 16th c.; *ROSS* |
| TAINSH | *MACGREGOR* |
| TAIT, TATE | Angus, Edinburgh 14th c., Orkney 16th c. |
| TARRELL, TARRILL | Ross-shire 14th c., to *MACINTOSH* |
| TASKER | Perthshire, Angus 17th c. |
| TAWSEON, TAWSE | From MACTAVISH |
| TAYLOR | Dumfries to Angus 13th c.; *CAMERON* |
| TELFER, TELFORD | Lanarkshire etc. 14th c. |
| TEMPLE | Midlothian, to E. Lothian 15th c. |
| TEMPLETON | N. Ayrshire (Irvine) 13th c. |
| TENNANT, TENNENT | W. Lothian 13th c., Stirling 14th c. |
| TERRAS, TERRIS | Moray (Tarras) 14th c. |
| TEVIOTDALE | Roxburghshire 13th c. |
| THAIN, THAYNE | Banffshire 15th c., Angus 16th c. |
| THALLON | S.W. Fife 16th c. |
| THIN | Lauderdale etc. 16th c. |
| THIRD | Aberdeen 16th c. etc. |
| THOM, THOMAS | Angus etc. 15th c.; *MACTHOMAS* |
| THOMASON | Sutherland 16th c.; *MACFARLANE* |
| THOMPSON | From THOMSON |
| THOMS | From *MACTHOMAS*; *MACINTOSH* |

| | |
|---|---|
| THOMSON | Ayrshire 14th c.; *MACTHOMAS* |
| THORBURN | Aberdeen 14th c., Tweeddale 15th c. |
| THORNTON | Mearns, also Angus 13th c. |
| THRIEPLAND | Peeblesshire 13th c., to Perth 17th c. |
| TINDALL, TINDELL | Dumfries, Glasgow 13th c., Angus 15th c. |
| TINLIN, TINLINE | Roxburghshire 17th c. |
| TOD, TODD | Berwickshire 13th c.; *GORDON* |
| TOFTS | C. Roxburghshire, (Kirkton) 13th c. |
| TOLMIE | *MACLEOD* of Lewis |
| TONNOCHY | *ROBERTSON* |
| TOPP | Aberdeenshire 15th c. |
| TORBAIN | Fife (Kirkcaldy) 16th c. |
| TORRANCE | N.W. Lanarkshire (Torrance) 16th c. |
| TORRIE, TORRY | Dumfriesshire 15th c.; *CAMPBELL* |
| TOSH, TOSHACH | *MACINTOSH* of Glentilt |
| TOSSACK | *MACGREGOR* |
| TOUCHE, TOUGH | Aberdeenshire 14th c., Fife 16th c. |
| TOWARD, TOWART | *LAMONT* |
| TOWERS | Edinburgh 14th c. |
| TOWNS | Edinburgh 15th c., Linlithgow 16th c. |
| TRAIL, TRAILL | Fife, Aberdeen 14th c., Orkney 16th c. |
| TRAIN | Ayrshire 15th c.; *MACDONALD* |
| TRAQUAIR | Peeblesshire 13th c. |
| TRENCH | Berwickshire 16th c. |
| TROTTER | Berwickshire and Edinburgh 14th c. |
| TROUP | Ayrshire 13th c., Banff 14th c.; *GORDON* |
| TUDHOPE | Jedburgh, to Lanark etc. 17th c. |
| TULLIS | Fife 16th c. |
| TULLOCH, TULLO | Angus etc. 14th c.; *ROSS* |
| TULLY, TULLIE | Aberdeenshire 16th c. etc. |
| TURCAN | W. Fife 17th c. |
| TURNBULL | Teviotdale etc. 14th c. |
| TURNER | Aberdeen 14th c., Ayrshire 15th c.; *LAMONT* |
| TURPIE, TURPIN | 'Thorfinn', Angus 13th c., Fife 17th c. |
| TWADDLE | From TWEEDDALE |
| TWATT | Orkney 16th c., also Shetland 17th c. |
| TWEEDDALE | Tweed 14th c.; *FRASER*; *HAY* |
| TWEEDIE, TWEEDY | Lanarkshire 13th c., Tweed 14th c.; *FRASER* |
| TYRE | From *MACINTYRE*, also MACTIRE |
| TYRIE | Perthshire 13th c., to Angus etc. 15th c. |
| | |
| UNDERWOOD | Ayrshire (Symington) 15th c. |
| URE | Midlothian 13th c.; also MACIVER |
| URIE, URRY | Clan *URQUHART* |
| URQUHART | Ayrshire, also Mearns 13th c.; *KEITH* |
| USHER | Angus 15th c., Peeblesshire 15th c. |
| | |
| VALENTINE | Kincardineshire 14th c. |
| VALLANCE | Angus 12th c., Fife 13th c. |
| VASS | E. Lothian 12th c.; *MUNRO*; *ROSS* |
| VEITCH, VETCH | Peeblesshire 13th c. |
| VERT, VERTH | Edinburgh 17th c. |
| VICKERS, VICARS | Roxburghshire 13th c. |
| | |
| WADDELL, WADDEL | Wedale (Stow) etc. 13th c. |
| WAITT, WAITE | Angus 14th c., Tweedside 16th c. |

| SURNAME | CLAN OR DISTRICT SOURCE |
|---------|------------------------|
| WAKE | Dumfriesshire 14th c., Edinburgh 15th c. |
| WALDIE, WADDIE | Kelso 12th c., Aberdeen 14th c. |
| WALKER | Galloway, Inverness etc. 14th c. Same as MACNUCATOR |
| WALKINGSHAW | Renfrewshire 13th c. |
| WALLACE, WALLIS | Ayrshire, Renfrewshire 12th c. |
| WALLS | Orkney 15th c.; also from WALLACE |
| WALSH | Same as WELSH |
| WALTER, WALTERS | Galloway, Fife, Aberdeen 14th c.; *BUCHANAN*; *FORBES* |
| WANLESS, WANLISS | W. Lothian 16th c., Angus 17th c. |
| WANN | Edinburgh, Glasgow etc. 15th c. |
| WARD | Peeblesshire 14th c., Stirling 17th c. |
| WARDEN | Angus, Fife etc. 17th c. |
| WARDLAW | Fife 11th c., Roxburghshire 14th c. |
| WARDROP | Fife and Midlothian 13th c. |
| WARE | Same as WEIR |
| WARES | N.E. Caithness; *SINCLAIR* |
| WARNOCK | 'Macilvernock', Galloway 12th c. |
| WARRACK | Aberdeenshire 15th c., Edinburgh 16th c. |
| WARREN | W. Fife 13th c. |
| WARWICK | Ayrshire etc. 13th c. |
| WASS | Same as VASS |
| WATERS | From WALTERS |
| WATERSTON | Angus, Midlothian etc. 14th c. |
| WATSON, WASON | *BUCHANAN*; *FORBES* |
| WATT, WATTERS | 'Walter': *FORBES*; *BUCHANAN* |
| WATTIE, WATTS | Aberdeenshire, *FORBES* |
| WAUCHOPE | Dumfriesshire, Midlothian 11th c. |
| WAUGH | From WAUCHOPE, Roxburghshire 13th c. |
| WEATHERHEAD | Lauderdale 15th c. |
| WEATHERSTONE | Lauderdale 17th c., from WATERSTON |
| WEBSTER, WEAVER | Stirling etc. 15th c.; *MACFARLANE* |
| WEDDELL, WEDDLE | Same as WADDELL |
| WEDDERBURN | Berwickshire 13th c., Dundee 15th c.; HOME; SCRIMGEOUR |
| WEIR | Lanarkshire 12th c.; and from MACNUIR |
| WELIVER | *MACGREGOR* |
| WELLS | Fife and Aberdeenshire 13th c. |
| WELSH, WELCH | Tweedside 14th c. |
| WEMYSS, WEEMS | Fife 12th c.; *MACDUFF* (Wemyss is now a clan in its own right) |
| WEST | Perthshire, Buchan etc. 17th c. |
| WESTON | Lanarkshire, Wigtown etc. 13th c. |
| WESTWATER | W. Fife 16th c. |
| WESTWOOD | Fife 15th c. |
| WHAMOND | 'Quhoman', Banff 15th c. |
| WHANNEL | Galloway, see MACWHANNELL |
| WHARRIE | Lanarkshire, from *MACQUARRIE* |
| WHEELAN, WHELLAN | Argyll 16th c.; *MACDONALD* |
| WHIGHAM | Peebles 15th c., Lothians 16th c. |
| WHITE, WHYTE | Angus 13th c., Ayrshire etc. 14th c.; *LAMONT*; *MACGREGOR* |
| WHITECROSS | Aberdeenshire 16th c. |
| WHITEFORD | Renfrewshire 13th c. |
| WHITEHEAD | Berwick 13th c., W. Lothian 16th c. |

| SURNAME | CLAN OR DISTRICT SOURCE |
|---|---|
| WHITELAW | Roxburghshire, Midlothian 13th c. |
| WHITSON | Perthshire 14th c., Angus 15th c. |
| WHITTEN, WHITTON | Roxburghshire 12th c. |
| WHYMAN | Peebles 14th c., and as WHAMOND |
| WHYTOCK | Edinburgh 16th c. |
| WIGHT | Perth 13th c., E. Lothian 16th c. |
| WIGHTMAN | Peeblesshire etc. 16th c. |
| WIGHTON | Angus 15th c. |
| WILCOX | *MACGREGOR* |
| WILKIE | Midlothian 14th c., also from MACQUILKAN |
| WILKINSON | Lanarkshire 15th c., also from MACQUILKAN |
| WILL, WILLS | Aberdeen 15th c.; *GUNN* |
| WILLIS, WILLISON | Dumfries 13th c., Lanarkshire 17th c. |
| WILLIAMSON | Fife 12th c., Peebles 14th c.; *MACKAY,* also from MACWILLIAM |
| WILLOCKS, WILLOX | Aberdeen 16th c.; also *MACGREGOR* |
| WILSON | Ayrshire etc. 15th c.; *GUNN* |
| WINDRAM, WINRAM | Lanarkshire 15th c., Fife etc. 16th c. |
| WINCHESTER | Ayrshire, Lanarkshire 13th c. |
| WINGATE, WINZET | Glasgow 16th c. |
| WINNING | Ayrshire etc. 13th c. |
| WINTON, WINTOUN | E. Lothian 12th c., Aberdeen etc. 14th c. |
| WINTOUR, WINTERS | Selkirkshire 12th c., Glasgow etc. 15th c. |
| WISEMAN | Moray 13th c., Aberdeenshire 14th c. |
| WISHART | Kincardineshire etc. 13th c. |
| WOOD | Nairnshire 13th c., Dumfriesshire 14th c. |
| WOODBURN | Ayrshire 16th c. |
| WORKMAN | Dunfermline 16th c. etc. |
| WOTHERSPOON | Renfrew 13th c., Fife etc. 16th c. |
| WRIGHT | Stirlingshire etc. 13th c.; *MACINTYRE* |
| WYATT | Angus 13th c. |
| WYLIE, WYLLIE | Dumfriesshire 14th c.; *GUNN*; *MACFARLANE* |
| WYSE | Moray etc. 14th c., Stirling 15th c. |
| | |
| YATES, YEATS | Dumfriesshire 14th c., Angus 15th c. |
| YEAMAN, YEOMAN | Moray, Dundee 16th c. |
| YELLOWLEES | Fife 15th c., Berwickshire 16th c. |
| YORKSTON, YORSTON | Edinburgh and Orkney 15th c. |
| YOUNG | Moray, Angus etc. 14th c. |
| YOUNGER | Fife etc. 14th c. |
| YOUNGSON | Aberdeenshire 16th c. |
| YOUNNIE, YUNNIE | Moray 17th c. |
| YOURSTON | From YORKSTON |
| YUILL, YULE, YOOL | Aberdeen etc. 14th c.; *BUCHANAN* |
| | |
| ZUILL | See YUILL, *BUCHANAN* |

# CLANS OF SCOTLAND

Alphabetically arranged, with lists of traditional septs and including the more common name variations and the names of dependent or associated families.


**Definition of the word 'Clan'**
The Gaelic word for 'children' is more accurately translated as 'family' in the sense in which the word *clan* became accepted in the Scottish Highlands during the 13th century. A clan is a social group whose core comprises a number of families derived from, or accepted as being derived from, a common ancestor. Almost without exception, that core is accompanied by a further number of dependent and associated families who have either sought the protection of the clan at some point in history or have been tenants or vassals of its chief. That chief is owed allegiance by all members of the clan, but ancient tradition nevertheless states that 'the Clan is above the Chief'. Although Gaelic has been supplanted by English in the Lowlands of Scotland for nearly a thousand years, it is an acceptable convention to refer to the great Lowland families, like the Douglases, as clans, although the heads of certain families, such as Bruce, prefer not to use the term.

Allegiance was generally given to a father's clan, but Celtic tradition includes a strong element of descent through, and loyalty to, a mother's line. In reality, the chief of a clan would 'ingather' any stranger — of whatever family — who possessed suitable skills, maintained his allegiance and, if required, adopted the clan surname.


**CLAN ALPIN**   Tradition claims MacAlpin or MacAlpine as the oldest and most purely Celtic of the Highland clans, of royal descent from the dynasty of Kenneth MacAlpin who united Picts and Scots into one kingdom from the year 850 and transferred his capital to Perthshire from Dun Add in Dalriada (beside Loch Crinan). However, no clan of the name survived into the heyday of the clan system, though individual MacAlpins are recorded from the 13th century, mostly then in Perthshire. Clan MacGregor claims origin from that royal MacAlpin stock: as also do MacAulay, MacDuff, MacFie, MacKinnon, MacNab and MacQuarrie.


**ARMSTRONG**          This variation of the Norman name Fortinbras has been known in the West Marches since the 13th century. Before the Union of the Crowns in 1603, this small border clan found themselves in an area of sharp contention, and the Armstrong chiefs adopted a traditional right of wide foray and tribute-levying into the 'Auld Enemy's' territory. At length, such diplomatic embarrassments from his over-active subjects moved James V to suppress them in 1529 by an expedition disguised as a great hunting tour. Several border ballads recount the aggrieved shock of 'Johnnie Armstrong of Gilknockie' and other leaders preparing to welcome their sovereign and finding themselves facing the hangman instead. That not all the clan were alike is obvious from the Gilbert Armstrong who was High Steward to King David II and his ambassador to England.

**Septs:**

| | | |
|---|---|---|
| CROSIER | FAIRBAIRN | NIXON |
| CROZER | GROZIER | |

**BRODIE**          Early records were destroyed by Lord Gordon, when he burned Brodie Castle, Nairnshire, in 1645; but the de Brothies or Brodies are elsewhere mentioned in influential positions from at least the 14th century. Whether an ancient tribe secured in loyal possession or related to the incoming Murrays, the Brodie name and lands became established when Malcolm IV transplanted other rebelling Moray tribes to different districts, about 1165.

**Septs:**

| BRODY | BRYDE | BRYDIE |
|---|---|---|

**BRUCE**          With the representatives of Norman families who accompanied William the Conqueror, those of de Brus, Robert and his two sons, were not far behind. In the name of Brusi, another branch directly Norse had already acquired a share of the Orkney earldom.

Robert's second son, Adam, acquired large territories in Yorkshire, and Adam's son Robert was one of the friends of the Scottish King David I who accompanied him at his accession in 1124, when returning from his sojourn in England. This Robert de Brus was granted the lordship of Annandale with the hand of that district's native heiress. The seventh of the Brus lords of Annandale, Robert de Brus (1274-1329, and later often called 'The Bruce'), was to become King Robert I, the victor of Bannockburn and liberator of Scotland.

From his mother, the heiress of Carrick, Turnberry Castle became a new nucleus of the Bruces; then from 1359 another branch spread still more extensively from Clackmannan into Fife and elsewhere. From Kinnaird, on the Forth shore opposite, came James Bruce (1730-94), who displayed gifts more versatile and diplomatic than are suggested by a bare reminder of his Abyssinian adventures and first exploration of the Nile sources.

**Septs:**

| CARLYLE | CROSBIE | STENHOUSE |
|---|---|---|
| CARRUTHERS | RANDOLPH | |

**BUCHANAN**          Legend derives the clan's original name MacAuslan from Irish prince Anselan O Kyan, granted a settlement in Lennox by Malcolm II. The Auselan first actually recorded was steward to a 13th-century Earl of Lennox, from whom he obtained the Loch-Lomondside district of Buchanan, which includes Ben Lomond. His son Gilbert was the first user of the Buchanan surname, as well as founder of the branches that took his name. From Gilbert's brothers Colman and Methlan, grandson Maurice and great-grandson Walter, there derived other sept names and the separated clan MacMillan.

George Buchanan, a forerunner (though in Latin) of Burns and Byron, the tutor of Montaigne, Mary Queen of Scots and James VI, historian and Reformationist, ranks as the clan's chief personality, though a U.S. President could be among others cited.

**Septs:**

| COLMAN | LENNIE | MACCHRUITER | MACKINLEY |
|---|---|---|---|
| CORMACK | LENNY | MACCOLMAN | MACMASTER |
| COUSLAND | MACALDONICH | MACCORMACK | MACMAURICE |
| DEWAR | MACALMAN | MACCUBBIN | MACMURCHIE |
| DOVE | MACASLAN | MACCUBING | MACMURCHY |
| DOW | MACASLIN | MACCUBIN | MACNEUR |
| GIBB | MACAUSELAN | MACGEORGE | MACNUIR |
| GIBBON | MACAUSLAN | MACGIBBON | MACNUYER |
| GIBSON | MACAUSLAND | MACGREUSICH | MACQUATTIE |
| GILBERT | MACAUSLANE | MACGUBBIN | MACWATTIE |
| GILBERTSON | MACCALMAN | MACINALLY | MACWHIRTER |
| HARPER | MACCALMONT | MACINDEOR | MASTERS |
| HARPERSON | MACCAMMOND | MACINDOE | MASTERSON |
| LEAVY | MACCASLAND | MACKINLAY | MORRICE |

| | | | |
|---|---|---|---|
| MORRIS | RUSK | WASON | YUILL |
| MORRISON | RUSKIN | WATERS | YOOL |
| MURCHIE | SPITTAL | WATSON | YULE |
| MURCHISON | SPITTEL | WATT | ZUILL |
| RICHARDSON | WALTER | WATTERS | |
| RISK | WALTERS | WEIR | |

**CAMERON**            The clan, settled in Lochaber since at least Bruce's time, later became an important branch of the Clan Chattan confederacy, and their name, taken as *Cam-shorn* ('s' silent), 'hook-nose', is reported to have fitted many Highland Camerons. But Camerons also, from the Norman name Cambron, had for a century before Bruce been spreading widely from their Fife headquarters of the same name. If the name in common is more coincidence, it is not the only one.

Among several branches of the Highland clan, that of the Chief acquired their Lochiel property by marriage and made that name, with their motto 'For King and Country', resound in the Stewart causes. Then in 1793 under Cameron of Erracht they founded the 79th or Cameron Highlanders to serve with no less distinction.

The southern Camerons of the 17th century directed their zeal rather differently. The scholarly John Cameron founded a protestant group in France called Cameronites; Richard Cameron, killed at Airdsmoss, 1680, a militant Covenanter, gave his name to the Cameronian sect and a later Lowland regiment.

**Septs:**

| | | | |
|---|---|---|---|
| CHALMERS | KENNEDY | MACILDOWIE | MACSORLEY |
| CHAMBERS | LEARY | MACKAIL | MACULRIG |
| CLARK | LONIE | MACKELL | MACVAIL |
| CLARKE | MACALDOWIE | MACLEAR | MACWALRICK |
| CLARKSON | MACALONIE | MACCLEARY | MARTIN |
| CLEARY | MACCHLERY | MACLERIE | PAUL |
| CLERK | MACCLAIR | MACMARTIN | SORLEY |
| DOWIE | MACLEARY | MACONIE | SORLIE |
| GIBBON | MACGILLERY | MACOSTRICH | TAYLOR |
| GILBERTSON | MACGILLONIE | MACPHAIL | |

**CAMPBELL**            Like their name itself, frequently interpreted as *Cambeul*, 'wry-mouth', this forthrightly ambitious clan claims origins both Celtic and Norman, though the accounts vary. One relates how Malcolm of the clan, anciently named O'Duibhne or MacDiarmid, went as a widower to Norman France where he married an heiress of the Beauchamp family and adopted that name. A son, Archibald, accompanied the Conqueror in 1066 and became founder to several English lines, these ringing changes on the name, as Beauchamp to Beecham, Campobello to Kemble. Hugo de Morville, David I's High Constable and assistant feudaliser, married Beatrix de Campobello and introuced Campbells as vassals on his Ayrshire lands.

Of their main stem, rising to its dukedom of Argyll, we hear of them in possession at Lochow (Loch Awe) after Alexander II's conquest of Argyll. This need not contradict the other tradition of Lochow as O'Duibhne territory from long earlier. It would clinch with the Campbell aptitude for backing the winning authority, and with their later royal commission of 1614-17 to suppress the refractory MacDonalds and oust them from Kintyre. The troublesome MacGregors of Perthshire had just previously been treated to a similar policing. And Highland memories run deep. Among many Campbell branches, that of Breadalbane illustrates their other aptitude for successful marriage, being begun by a 14th-century match with the Glenorchy heiress. For other septs, see Campbell of Cawdor, also MacArthur.

Thomas Campbell (1777-1844) was author of many rousing ballads, including 'Lochiel's Warning', 'Lord Ullin's Daughter', and 'Battle of the Baltic'.

## Septs:

| | | | |
|---|---|---|---|
| BALLANTYNE | KISSOCK | MACGLASRICH | MACORAN |
| BANNATYNE | LORNE | MACGUBBIN | MACPHEDRAN |
| BURNES | LOUDEN | MACISAAC | MACQUAKER |
| BURNESS | LOWDON | MACIVER | MACTAUSE |
| BURNS | LOWDEN | MACIVOR | MACTAVISH |
| CONNOCHIE | LOUDON | MACKELLAR | MACTHOMAS |
| CONOCHIE | MACCOLM | MACKELVIE | MACURE |
| DENOON | MACCOMBE | MACKERLICH | MACVICAR |
| DENUNE | MACCONACHIE | MACKERLIE | OCHILTREE |
| DONACHIE | MACCONCHIE | MACKESSACK | ORR |
| DONAGHY | MACCONNECHY | MACKESSOCK | PATERSON |
| FISHER | MACCURE | MACKISSOCK | PINKERTON |
| HAWES | MACDERMID | MACKIVER | TAWESON |
| HAWS | MACDERMONT | MACLAWS | TAWSE |
| HAWSON | MACDIARMID | MACLEHOSE | THOMAS |
| ISAAC | MACDONACHIE | MACLIVER | THOMPSON |
| ISAACS | MACELLAR | MACNICHOL | THOMSON |
| IVERSON | MACELVIE | MACNICOL | URE |
| KELLAR | MACEUR | MACNIVEN | |
| KELLER | MACEVER | MACNOCAIRD | |
| KISSACK | MACGIBBON | MACONACHIE | |

**CAMPBELL of Cawdor**      The Calder or Cawdor family and name derive from Hugh de Cadella and his heirs, who gave valuable service to King Malcolm Canmore and his successors and were awarded the Nairnshire thaneship which is notably mentioned in Shakespeare's *Macbeth*. In 1493 this fell to an infant heiress, Muriel, and James IV appointed as wards her uncle, a Rose of Kilravock, and the Earl of Argyll. The latter sent an expedition which contrived to abduct Muriel as a young child to Inveraray, where in 1510 she married the Earl's third son, Sir John Campbell, and thus gave that clan a northern foothold.

## Septs:

| | | |
|---|---|---|
| CADDELL | CALDER | TORRIE |
| CADELL | CATTELL | TORRY |

**CLAN CHATTAN**    This long-powerful group of clans comprised two main divisions, respectively under Macintosh and MacPherson leadership, with some subsidiary septs and family groups joining for protection under a geneal banner. Dissension arose among the sections from various causes, not least from their encroaching neighbours, the Gordons, enticing them into opposing camps, as at Harlaw in 1411.

Accounts of the Clan Chattan's origin vary. The Macintoshes, holding to their own Macduff origin, regard it as a confederacy, with the MacPhersons just a branch from Macintosh stock. MacPhersons, putting reliance on a written genealogy of 1450, favour the Chattan sections as having branched from an ancestor, Gillechattan Mor, a Moray chief of the early 11th century, his elder son Nechtan founding the MacPhersons and the younger, Neil, the Macintoshes, which surname only appears two centuries later. Either way of it, the Clunie MacPhersons retained the old Chattan chiefship, although in 1291 the Macintoshes, through marriage of their chief Angus to Eva, the MacPherson heiress, achieved the greater share of land and followers and also their chief's right to be styled 'Captain of the Clan Chattan', leaving their claim to full chiefship a good-going dispute scarcely yet settled.

**Septs:**

| **MacPherson Group** | **Macintosh Group** | |
|---|---|---|
| MACPHERSON | MACINTOSH | MACHARDIE |
| DAVIDSON | FARQUHARSON | MACQUEEN |
| GILLESPIE | MACBEAN | NOBLE |
| KEITH | MACGILLIVRAY | MACTAVISH |
| SMITH | MACGLASHAN | SHAW |

Also: CAMERON, CATTANACH, CLARK, MACPHAIL

**CHISHOLM**          Originally Normans, the Chisholm or Chisholme family took name from the lands of Chesholm that they occupied in Roxburghshire from the 13th century or earlier. It was through marriages with northern heiresses that they established themselves a Highland clan, and Sir Robert de Chesholme became in 1359 Constable of the royal castle of Urquhart. Erchless Castle, Strathglass, remains the ancestral seat of their chief.

**COLQUHOUN**          The lands of Colquhoun (pronounced 'Cohoon') by Loch Lomond, were granted by a 13th-century Earl of Lennox to Humphrey de Kilpatrick or Kirkpatrick, from whom the clan take descent. In the following century the neighbouring lands of Luss were included through Sir Robert Colquhoun's marrying their heiress. The last inter-clan battle, in Glenfruin nearby, in 1603, was the culmination of the long feud between the Colquhouns and MacGregors and led to the outlawry of the latter by royal command.

**Septs:**

| | | | |
|---|---|---|---|
| COWAN | KIRKPATRICK | MACCOWAN | MACMANUS |
| COWEN | LAING | MACLINDEN | MACOWAN |
| INGRAM | MACACHOUNICH | MACLINTOCK | |
| KILPATRICK | MACCLINTOCK | MACMAINS | |

**CUMMING**          The Cummings or Cumyns trace Norman descent from Charlemagne through Robert de Comyn, appointed governor of Northumberland in 1068 by his kinsman, William the Conqueror. Under David I, William de Comyn became Chancellor of Scotland in 1133. Settled first in Roxburghshire, the family later gained through marriages the earldoms of Buchan and Badenoch, and Altyre in Moray has long been the seat of their chief. From 1309 the Comyns' power was broken through their having contested Bruce's succession to the throne. Sir John ('the Red') Comyn's mother was the sister of ex-king John Baliol. He was slain by Bruce's party at Dumfries, and the Buchan Comyns were defeated in battle at Inverurie, 1308.

**Septs:**

| | | | |
|---|---|---|---|
| BUCHAN | COMMON | CUMMINGS | MACNIVEN |
| CHEYNE | COMMONS | CUMYN | NIVEN |
| CHIENE | CUMMIN | FARQUHARSON | RUSSELL |

**DAVIDSON**          The clan MacDhai or Davidson, earliest settled at Invernahaven in Strathspey, are believed to take name from an ancestor, David Dhu, fourth son of Murriach, the 12th-century founder of the MacPhersons. Members of the Clan Chattan, they were deeply involved in the quarrels of precedency that beset that confederacy. These were publicly culminated in 1396 in the famous thirty-a-side combat MacPherson v. Davidson, before King Robert III and his court on the North Inch of Perth. Whether because 29 leading MacDhais were killed, or because one escaped alive, the clan thereafter fell from prominence. They are now chiefly represented by the Davidsons of Tulloch in Cromarty. A small border clan Davidson arose in Roxburghshire around the 16th century, perhaps of quite independent origin, like the Davie name in Orkney, and others. The Inverness-shire MacKays are really MacDhais.

**Septs:**

| | | | |
|---|---|---|---|
| DAVEY | DEA | DOW | MACDADE |
| DAVIE | DEAN | DYE | MACDAID |
| DAVIS | DEANE | KAY | MACDAVID |
| DAVISON | DEAS | KEAY | MACKAY |
| DAWSON | DEASON | KEY | SLORA |
| DAY | DEY | KEYS | SLORACH |

# DOUGLAS

An adequate history of the Douglases would be largely one of Scotland itself, where they long rivalled the royal power and eleven times married into it. Perhaps originally kinsmen of Freskin, the Clan Murray founder, it is in the south that they first come to note. Here in the 12th century they originated the 'Black Douglases' — of Douglasdale (Lanarkshire), Dumfriesshire, and Galloway. The next century saw the 'Red Douglases' established at Dalkeith (whence sprang the Earls of Morton), and then in Angus. The term 'Black Douglas' was first applied by the English to the Sir James who was Bruce's doughty lieutenant, to fall at last in Spain when on his final service of conveying the royal heart to the Holy Land.

**Septs:**

| | | | |
|---|---|---|---|
| CAVERS | FORREST | LOCKERBY | SANDILANDS |
| DOUGLASS | GLENDINNING | MACGUFFIE | |
| DRYSDALE | INGLIS | MACGUFFOCK | |
| FOREST | KIRKPATRICK | MORTON | |

# DRUMMOND

The name is from the clan's earliest land at Drymen, near Loch Lomond, conferred, a tradition says, upon their ancestor Maurice who married Queen Margaret's maid-of-honour; adding that either he or his father was the Hungarian prince who piloted the refugee vessel of 1066 that brought Malcolm Canmore's bride-to-be. The earliest chief now documented was Malcolm Beg, or 'the little', a 13th-century Steward to the Earl of Lennox.

The Drummond arms display a motto, 'Gang warily', and the caltrops, those four-spiked cavalry snags that a later Sir Malcolm contributed to the victory of Bannockburn. For his services, Bruce awarded the lands in Perthshire where chiefly the clan was to flourish. Annabella Drummond became Queen to Robert II, the first Stewart king; and from then on to the last Stewart, no clan remained more faithfully adherent than the Drummonds.

**Septs:**

| | | | |
|---|---|---|---|
| BEGG | GREWAR | MACGROUTHER | MACROBIE |
| BREWER | GRUAR | MACGRUDER | MUSHET |
| CARGILL | GRUER | MACGRUER | ROBBIE |
| DOCK | MACCROUTHER | MACGRUTHER | |
| DOIG | MACGREWAR | MACROBBIE | |

# ELLIOT

The surname appears in the 13th century, both in England (from the Old English forename Elwald) and in Scotland at Arbirlot (Aber-Eliot). Induced by the Douglases about 1395 to remove from their Angus riverside and strengthen the Border in Liddesdale, the Elliots became from there a wide-spreading clan. The names varied with different branches, as the Elliots of Minto and Eliotts of Stobs. Gilbert Elliot (1751-1814), first Earl Minto, was among the greatest of India's governors-general. His Jacobite aunt Jane Elliot penned the Flodden lament 'The Flowers o' the Forest'.

## FARQUHARSON

A branch of Clan Chattan, the Aberdeenshire Farquharsons or MacEarachers descend from Farquhar, son of the Shaw Macintosh of Rothiemurchus, Strathspey, who was awarded lands in Braemar by Bruce for assistance against the northern Comyns. No such motive could be ascribed the clan for their devotion to the Stewart causes in after centuries. From Farquhar's grandson Finlay comes MacKinlay and some other sept names. The clan extended well into Perthshire, but MacEarachers etc. of around Argyll are of Lamont or other origin.

**Septs:**

| | | | |
|---|---|---|---|
| BARRIE | FINDLAY | KERRACHER | MACHARDIE |
| BOWMAN | FINDLAYSON | LYON | MACHARDY |
| CHRISTIE | FINLAISON | MACARTNEY | MACKERCHAR |
| CHRISTISON | FINLAY | MACCAIG | MACKERRACHER |
| CHRISTY | FINLAYSON | MACCARDNEY | MACKINDLAY |
| COATES | GRACIE | MACCARTNEY | MACKINLAY |
| COATS | GRASSICK | MACCUAIG | MACKINLEY |
| COUTTS | GREUSACH | MACEARACHER | PATERSON |
| CROMAR | HARDIE | MACERCHAR | REIACH |
| FARQUHAR | HARDY | MACERRACHER | REOCH |
| FERRIES | KELLAS | MACFARQUHAR | RIACH |

## FERGUSON

Fergus was the favourite name in Gaelic-speaking Scotland, after the founder of Dalriada (now roughly Argyll).

MacFerguses, Fergus-sons, or Fergusons thus arose in areas widely dispersed. The Ayrshire Fergussons probably take name, and perhaps descent, from Fergus, the wellnigh independent 12th-century lord of Galloway; they were certainly established in the southwest before their charter from Bruce. Annie Laurie of the song became the wife of a Dumfriesshire Fergusson. Robert Fergusson (1750-74), a forerunner and inspirer of Burns, came of the Aberdeenshire clan, known there since the 14th century; and his contemporary, Adam Ferguson, the social historian, was of the Atholl branch.

**Septs:**

| | | | |
|---|---|---|---|
| FERGIE | FERRIES | KIDDIE | MACKEDDIE |
| FERGUS | FORGIE | MACADIE | MACKERRAS |
| FERGUSSON | KEDDIE | MACFERGUS | MACKERSEY |

## FORBES

In its Aberdeenshire home the name is still pronounced with two syllables and is from the lands of Forbois or Forbes, granted by Alexander III to one Duncan. His son Alexander de Forbes was slain in 1304 after a long defence of Urquhart Castle (Moray) against Edward I; and his son, also Alexander, in 1332 at Dupplin Moor. Duncan Forbes (1685-1747), Lord President of the Court of Session and skilful opponent to both Jacobite rebellions from a patriotism no less sincere, matched cool wisdom against impulsive ardour and tempered justice with all the mercy he could wring from a prejudiced government.

**Septs:**

| | | | |
|---|---|---|---|
| BANNERMAN | LUMSDEN | MEKIE | WATERS |
| BERRIE | MACOUAT | MELDRUM | WATSON |
| BERRY | MACOWAT | MICHIE | WATT |
| BOYCE | MACQUATTIE | MIDDLETON | WATTERS |
| BOYES | MACWATT | WALTER | WATTIE |
| FORDYCE | MECHIE | WALTERS | WATTS |

# FRASER

At first de Friselle or Fresel, then 'Fraisier' from the *fraises*, or strawberry flowers, in their armorial bearings, this Norman family first settled in Tweeddale under Malcolm Canmore to become the chief power in Peeblesshire throughout the 12th and 13th centuries, owning Oliver, Neidpath and other castles, also estates in East Lothian. The chief male line there dying out, it devolved upon the Lovat branch which had firmly established itself in the north in Bruce's time. A further branch of Philorth founded Fraserburgh in the 16th century.

The Fraser clan have played a full part in history, not only in Scotland. For his Jacobite activities, Simon Fraser (Lord Lovat) was beheaded after Culloden at the age of eighty; and a later namesake explored the Fraser river of Canada. Sir James Frazer, author of *The Golden Bough*, made folklore a study of the modern scientist.

**Septs:**

| | | | |
|---|---|---|---|
| ABERNETHY | GILRUTH | MACKIMMIE | SIMS |
| BISSET | GREWAR | MACSIMON | SIMSON |
| BISSETT | GRUAR | MACSYMON | SYM |
| BREWSTER | GRUER | MACTAVISH | SYME |
| COWIE | MACGREWAR | OLIVER | SYMON |
| FRAZER | MACGRUER | SIM | SYMONS |
| FRESER | MACILLRICK | SIME | TWADDLE |
| FREZEL | MACILRIACH | SIMON | TWEEDDALE |
| FRISELL | MACIMMEY | SIMONS | TWEEDIE |
| FRIZELLE | MACKIM | SIMPSON | |

# GAYRE

of Gayre and Nigg arose in Cornwall in the 12th century. One branch settled in Yorkshire in the 15th century and crossed into Scotland in the 16th century and held lands in Nigg in Ross-shire. They rapidly multiplied and became landowners throughout Easter Ross. A small clan, it was recognised by Lord Lyon earlier this century.

**Septs:**

| | | | |
|---|---|---|---|
| GAIR | GAYRE | MCGAIR | GARSON |
| GAIRE | GAIRN | MCGEIR | KERRISON |
| GEAR | GEIR | GARRISON | MCGIRR |

# GORDON

The 'Gay Gordons', also the name Huntly, had their Scottish origin in the Berwickshire lands of Gordon. Here, as a Norman family, they became settled under David I and retained estates for three centuries. Sir Adam de Gordon was one of the ambassadors who conveyed to the Pope the 1320 Declaration of National Independence, the first of its kind. For this and other services, Bruce granted him land of the forfeited Cummings at Strathbogie in Aberdeenshire. From that centre the Gordons came to exert great power (their chief was often called 'The Cock of the North') and were much in feud with neighbouring clans, quite often on the side of governmental stability. They founded in 1777 and 1794 the regiments that became the Gordon Highlanders.

Individuals have achieved mark in many ways, as 'Chinese Gordon', slain at Khartoum in 1885, and Lord Byron, the poet of freedom and love, a Gordon on his mother's side. Three Gordons have separately compiled works treasured for depicting Old Scotland, such as her first great Atlas of 1654.

**Septs:**

| | | | |
|---|---|---|---|
| ADAM | ADIE | ATKINS | CROMB |
| ADAMS | AITCHISON | ATKINSON | CROMBIE |
| ADAMSON | AIKEN | BARRIE | CULLEN |
| ADDIE | AITKEN | CONNON | DARG |
| ADDISON | ATKIN | CRAIG | DARGE |

| | | | |
|---|---|---|---|
| DORWARD | GARRICK | LAWRIE | MOIR |
| DUFF | GARRIOCK | LENG | MORE |
| DURWARD | GEDDES | MARR | MORRICE |
| EADIE | GERRIE | MAVER | MORRIS |
| EDDIE | HUNTLY | MAVOR | MUIR |
| EDIE | JESSIMAN | MELDRUM | MYLNE |
| EDISON | JOPP | MILL | TOD |
| ESSLEMONT | JUPP | MILLS | TODD |
| GARDINER | LAING | MILN | TROUP |
| GARDNER | LANG | MILNE | |
| GARIOCH | LAURIE | MILNES | |

## GRAHAM

William de Graham, perhaps a native Scot, was granted by David I the Lothian lands of Abercorn and Dalkeith. His great-grandson Henry, marrying the Eskdale heiress of Avenel, established a contingent on the west Border, though the direct line died out there. The Montrose branch sprang from a different grandson of William, Sir David de Graham, who settled in Angus under William the Lion. His eldest son acquired by marriage the Strathearn district that gave name to the Menteith branch. This is unconnected with Wallace's supposed betrayer, who at least did sign the 1320 Declaration of Independence, besides three Grahams.

The 'Gallant Grahams' often enter Scottish history, most notably in the 17th century when 'the Great Marquis' (Montrose) and 'Bonnie Dundee', forty years apart, each led valorously, and met death in, the royalist cause.

**Graham of Montrose Septs:**

| | | |
|---|---|---|
| BONAR | BONNAR | GRAHAME |

**Graham of Menteith Septs:**

| | | | |
|---|---|---|---|
| AIRTH | BUNTAIN | MACGIBBON | MONTEITH |
| ALLARDYCE | BUNTING | MACGILVERNOCK | PYE |
| BLAIR | GRAHAME | MACGRIME | PYOTT |
| BONTEIN | HADDEN | MENTEITH | |
| BONTINE | HALDANE | MONTEATH | |

## GRANT

Despite Gaelic interpretations, the name is simply from the French *Grand*, either 'Big' or 'Eminent', and the family was known in their original Normandy with the motto 'Stand fast!' Introduced to Scotland by marriage with the Inverness-shire Bissets, Gregory le Grant was Sheriff of that territory before 1250 and laird in Stratherrick, northeast of Loch Ness, whilst his son Lawrence, by marrying a Comyn heiress, acquired Strathspey lands that thereafter became their home country. The Glenmoriston branch was a 16th-century offshoot; and they, as indeed most of the clan, Norman in name only, adhered loyally to the Stewarts, though the Grant chiefs always favoured the ruling government.

Of General Ulysses Grant, U.S. President 1868-76, it was wagered his 'poker face' could not be tricked into emotion. But when a clansman called the old slogan 'Stand fast, Craigellachie!' (a Speyside crag), the forfeit had to be surrendered, with smiles all round.

**Septs:**

| | | | |
|---|---|---|---|
| ALLAN | BUIE | MACILROY | SUTTIE |
| BISSET | GILROY | MACKERRON | |
| BISSETT | MACALLAN | MACKIARAN | |
| BOWIE | MACGILROY | PRATT | |

**GUNN**          Though largely a Pictish tribe, the name probably equivalent to the Welsh 'Gwynn', the clan Gunn chiefs claimed Norse descent from one Gunni, son of a 12th-century Orcadian Olaf, acquiring Caithness lands from his mother's side, the Earls of Ross. A turbulent clan much in feud with the Keiths and MacKays, they found it advisable in the 15th century to move from Caithness to the Kildonan district of Sutherland. The sept names derive mostly from chief's sons as Johnson, MacIan, Mackean, Kean, Keene, all from 'son of John'. James (or Hamish), John, Henry (Eanrick), Rob and Will were all sons of the same 14th-century George Gunn, the 'Crowner' (royal legal deputy), William, of a later chief.

**Septs:**

| | | | |
|---|---|---|---|
| ENRICK | KEAN | MACOMISH | ROBSON |
| GALDIE | KEENE | MACROB | SANDISON |
| GALLIE | MACCOMAS | MACWILLIAM | SWAN |
| GANSON | MACCORKILL | MAGNUS | SWANN |
| GAULDIE | MACCORKLE | MAIN | SWANNEY |
| GAUNSON | MACCULLIE | MANN | SWANSON |
| GEORGESON | MACIAN | MANSON | WILL |
| HENDERSON | MACKAMES | MANUS | WILLIAMSON |
| INRIG | MACKEAMISH | NEILSON | WILLS |
| JAMESON | MACKEAN | NELSON | WILSON |
| JAMIESON | MACMAINS | ROBINSON | WYLIE |
| JOHNSON | MACMANUS | ROBISON | WYLLIE |

**HAY**          Hays have held ranks in France and elsewhere from early times. Several accompanied William the Conqueror in 1066; and a century later a descendant from these, William de la Haya, appears as cup-bearer to Malcolm IV and progenitor of the many branches of the Scottish clan. His elder son, William, became ancestor to the Earls of Errol; his younger, Robert, to the Yester branch and Marquises of Tweeddale. After Bannockburn, Bruce awarded Sir Gilbert Hay of Errol the Aberdeenshire lands of Slains and the hereditary High Constableship of Scotland.

**Septs:**

| CONSTABLE | GIFFORD | MACKESTER |
|---|---|---|

**HOME**          The name, properly pronounced 'Hume' and frequently so spelt, comes from the lands in Berwickshire acquired in marriage by a 13th-century descendant of the Northumbrian Earl Gospatrick, ancestor also of the Dunbars. By further marriages the Homes extended widely over the east Borderland and took full share in its wars and forays. David Hume (1711-76), philosopher-historian and indirect inspirer of many efforts to bring logic into practical history, also John Home, minister unfrocked for producing his poetic drama *Douglas* in 1756, might both claim family predecessors. Lord Kames, the lawyer-philosopher, and Lady Grizel Baillie, the balladist, were likewise born of the clan sometimes named 'the Haughty Homes'.

**Septs:**

| | | | |
|---|---|---|---|
| AYTON | EATON | LANDELS | WEDDERBURN |
| BUNCLE | GREENLAW | MACK | |
| BUNKLE | HALIBURTON | NESBITT | |
| DUNBAR | LANDALE | NISBET | |

**INNES**          The name is from Gaelic *Innis*, an inch or islet, being one near Elgin on lands granted to the Innes' ancestor Berowald in 1154 by Malcolm IV for service against the rebelling Moray tribes of that time. While later branches extended to other districts, all were noted for loyalty in the Stewart causes.

**Septs:**

| INCH | MACROB | REIDFURD |
|---|---|---|

**JOHNSTON**      John, a 12th-century holder of Annandale lands under the Bruces, gave name to his citadel or 'toun', from which his son took the surname de Johnston or Johnstone, the spelling indicating no real difference, though the 'e' is less frequent in north than south. A turbulent Border clan — hardly 'the Gentle Johnstones' to their Maxwell and Douglas rivals — they were frequently appointed Wardens of the West March, hence their motto 'Aye Ready'. The Aberdeenshire branch was founded by a 14th-century Steven de Johnston, from the Annandale family, marrying a Garrioch heiress. Johnstones of Coll are properly MacIans from Ardnamurchan, whilst occasional others have had the name as hailing from Perth, otherwise St John's-toun.

**Septs:**

| | | | |
|---|---|---|---|
| JOHNSTONE | MARCHBANKS | MARJORIBANKS | ROME |

**KEITH**      In the time of David I, Hervey de Keith possessed half of the lands named Keith in southwest East Lothian, and his great-grandson acquired the other half by marrying its Fraser heiress. As hereditary Grand Marischals of Scotland, the chiefs took a prominent part in the country's affairs and battles, and attained vast possessions, principally northwards. About 1390, Sir William Keith was the builder of historic Dunottar Castle as his main seat; and in 1593 the fifth Earl Marischal founded the famous Marischal College of Aberdeen. The tenth and last Earl forfeited title and all estates for active support of the Old Chevalier in 1715. The numerous Dicksons of the Border and Dixons in England descend from one of the early Keiths-Marischal.

**Septs:**

| | | | |
|---|---|---|---|
| AUSTIN | DIXSON | HERVEY | MARSHALL |
| DICKISON | FALCONER | HURRIE | URIE |
| DICKSON | HARVEY | HURRY | URRY |
| DIXON | HAXTON | LUMGAIR | |

**KENNEDY**      A genealogist has suggested the name to mean 'a kinsman', Henry Cinnidh or Kennedy being a younger brother of William the Lion and founder of this great Carrick clan. From supporting Bruce against the Comyns and James II against the Black Douglases, the Kennedies acquired great power in the land, albeit rocked by a centuries-long feud for seniority between the Bargany and Cassillis branches. One chief, the Earl of Cassillis in Mary's reign (and fighter in her cause), even ventured on the unofficial title 'King of Carrick'. Branches spread into Lennox in the 13th century, and Aberdeenshire in the 14th. The learned Bishop James Kennedy (and his daughter Kate) are still celebrated annually by the students of St Andrews University, where he founded a college in 1455.

**Septs:**

| | | | |
|---|---|---|---|
| CARRICK | CASSELS | CASSILLIS | MACWALRICK |

**KERR**      The Scottish Kers, Cars or Kerrs are recorded in Border history from the 12th century, after Normans of the name had been established in England from the Conquest. Though with offshoots reaching Ayrshire and Aberdeen by the 13th century, their main ground was Roxburghshire. There the Kerrs were early Sheriffs, and the principal divisions of the family became Kers of Cessford, of whom the Duke of Roxburgh is now chief, and Kerrs of Ferniehirst, now represented by the Marquess of Lothian.

**Septs:**

| | | | |
|---|---|---|---|
| CARR | CARRE | CESSFORD | KER |

**LAMONT**            The Clan MacEarcher (i.e. from some Farquhar chief, earlier than the northern Farquharsons' ancestor) were the immemorial of their part of Argyllshire, centred on Castle Toward in Cowal. A chief or his son in the 13th century seemingly acquired a special judicial rank that earned the clan, or its earliest branch, the new name 'Law-man', hence Laumon, Lamont and other variations. The clan lost power and territory to Campbells and other neighbours through marriages and less gentle means. A Dunoon monument recalls the 1646 capture and destruction of Toward Castle, with the subsequent massacre of many principal Lamonts on the excuse of their adherence to the royalist cause. The chief's seat thereafter became Ardlamont, at the other end of the Kyles of Bute.

**Septs:**

| | | | |
|---|---|---|---|
| BLACK | LAMOND | MACERCHAR | MACMUNN |
| BLACKIE | LAMONDSON | MACERRACHER | MACPATRICK |
| BLAIK | LEMMON | MACFARQUHAR | MACPHUN |
| BLAIKIE | LEMOND | MACGILLEDOW | MACSORLEY |
| BLAKE | LIMOND | MACGORRIE | MEIKLEHAM |
| BROUN | LIMONT | MACILDOWIE | MEIKLEM |
| BROWN | LUCAS | MACILWHOM | MUNN |
| BURDEN | LUCK | MACKERCHAR | PATERSON |
| BURDON | LUCKIE | MACKERRACHER | PATRICK |
| CLEMENT | LUKE | MACLAMOND | SORLEY |
| DOUGLAS | MACALDOWIE | MACLEMON | TOWARD |
| FORSYTH | MACALDUIE | MACLUCAS | TOWART |
| LAMB | MACCLEMENT | MACLUCKIE | TURNER |
| LAMBIE | MACCLYMONT | MACLUKE | WHITE |
| LAMMIE | MACEARACHER | MACLYMONT | WHYTE |

**LESLIE**            The name is from the lands of Leslie in Garrioch, Aberdeenshire, granted to Malcolm, son of Bartholf or Bartholomew, under King William the Lion. A 13th-century descendant obtained grant of the Fife lands now also called Leslie; and a later marriage brought to the family the earldom of Rothes in Moray, now seat of the chief. John Leslie (1526-96), Bishop of Ross, was a notable historian and devoted champion to Mary Queen of Scots. Then in the following century there were at one time active three Generals Leslie: Walter, Count Leslie, with the German Emperor, whilst Alexander and David Leslie both earned distinction first with Gustavus Adolphus, then with Scotland's Covenanting armies.

**Septs:**            ABERNETHY            LESSLIE            MORE

**LINDSAY**            The widespread Lindsays claim Norman origin, the name from an 'Isle of lime-trees' near Rouen and said to have been spelt nearly 200 different ways, as Limesay, Lindesey etc. in England. Under David I, Sir Walter Lindsay was the first to hold position in Scotland, the family settling by Tweedside, from Earlston to Caddonlea. Connected from the 12th century with Crawford on Upper Clyde (hence their chief earldom title), by the 14th they had extended by marriage to Fife and Angus. 'The Lindsays light and gay' — and some who were neither — took high rank in Scotland's affairs and battles. Sir David Lindsay of the Mount, tutor to King James V, could infuse gaiety into the reforming courage of his great drama of 1540, *The Three Estates*. The Lord Lindsay of 1740 was the first Colonel of the Black Watch regiment.

**Septs:**

| | | | |
|---|---|---|---|
| BUYERS | CRAWFORD | DOWNIE | RHYND |
| BYERS | DEUCHAR | FOTHERINGHAM | SUMMERS |
| COBB | DEUCHARS | RHIND | SUMNER |

**MACALISTER**　　　　　The ancestor to this earliest offshoot from the great Clan Donald was Allister (or Alexander), eldest son of Angus, Lord of the Isles and Kintyre. Through joining the MacDougalls against Robert Bruce, Alister forfeited his succession to that lordship, but his descendants, inhabiting a tract of Knapdale and North Kintyre, grew strong enough to extend into Arran and Bute and became an independent clan when the Lords of the Isles were suppressed in 1493. Their first Knapdale stronghold of Castle Sweyn was assaulted by Bruce, whereafter the chief's seat became Ardpatrick, and finally Loup in Kintyre. Though having lost much of its territory and strength to the Campbells, the clan appeared in the royalist ranks with Montrose, and again at Killiecrankie.

| **Septs:** | | | |
|---|---|---|---|
| | ALASTAIR | ALLISON | MACALLISTER |
| | ALEXANDER | ALLISTER | SANDERS |
| | ALISON | MACALASTER | SAUNDERS |

**MACARTHUR**　　　　　This early branch of the Campbell clan long claimed its chiefship. The Argyllshire MacArthurs of Bruce's time took their part against the MacDougalls of Lorne and were richly rewarded out of the latter's territory, including the custodianship of Dunstaffnage Castle. Their own too-ambitious power was broken in 1427 when John MacArthur, their chief, forfeited to King James I all clan territory and his own head to the block. The clan afterwards acquired footings at Strachur in Cowal and around Glendochart, whilst a sept of them were hereditary pipers to the MacDonalds of the Isles.

**Septs:**

| ARTHUR | CAMPBELL | MACCAIRTER | MACINDEOR |
|---|---|---|---|
| ARTHURSON | DEWAR | MACCARTER | |

**MACAULAY**　　　　　The Dunbartonshire Macaulays claim descent from MacGregor and hence MacAlpin stock. Seated at Ardincaple (now Helensburgh) since at least the 13th century, they were under protection of and closely connected with the old Earls of Lennox. It is from a brother, Aulay, of the Earl in Alexander II's time that the clan name is believed to derive. A branch that removed to Loch Fyne took the name MacPhedran, which became Paterson.

Lord Macaulay (1800-59), writer and statesman but famed chiefly for his *History of England*, was descended of a different small clan that was settled at Uig, on the west side of the Isle of Lewis. Of Norse origin, the name here deriving from 'Olaf', these Northern Macaulays were often at feud with the neighbouring Morrisons and usurping MacKenzies.

| **Septs of the** | | | |
|---|---|---|---|
| **Lennox clan:** | MACALL | MACKELL | MACPHEIDRAN |
| | MACCALL | MACPHEDRAN | PATERSON |
| | MACKAIL | MACPHEDRON | PATTERSON |
| **Septs of either clan:** | | AULAY | MACAULLY |
| | | MACALLEY | MACCAULEY |

**MACBEAN**　　　　　This clan in Moray was one of the Clan Chattan confederacy. Although in the 'Forty-five' they served with gallantry under Lochiel, normally they followed the Macintosh banner, their founder having arrived in the suite of the 1291 MacPherson heiress who married the Macintosh chief. Originally they claim common stock with the Macbeths, from that 11th-century king of Scotland.

**Septs:**

| BEAN | MACBEATH | MACILVEEN | MACVEAN |
|---|---|---|---|
| BINNIE | MACBETH | MACVAIN | |
| MACBAIN | MACILVAIN | MACVANE | |

C

**MACBETH**          One of the exceptions among the 'Macs', the name means not the son of any person 'Beth', but 'Son of life', or a man of religion. It developed a separate form Macbean (see above), and has also become confused with forms of the Norman name Bethune. Shakespeare, playing his immortal light over the old Celtic throne of Scotland, brings to focus the ruler of Moray who enforced his family claim thereon by the murder of King Duncan in 1040. Macbeths, frequently called Beatons, held high repute and rank from the 14th century to the 17th, as physicians and chancellors to the MacDonalds of Islay and Macleans of Mull, sometimes also to royalty and elsewhere.

## Septs:

| | | | |
|---|---|---|---|
| BEATON | BEATTY | BETHUNE | MACBHEATH |
| BEATTIE | BELTON | LEITCH | MACBHEATH |

## MACDONALD (of the Isles):
## CLAN DONALD NORTH
## CLAN DONALD SOUTH

Greatest and most widespread of all, Clan Donald has its main roots in the old Gaelic and Pictish times, with additions from the Norsemen just when the curtain of history begins lifting on personalities. There is a legendary ancestor, Conn of the Battles, but the first clear one is Somerled, the thane of Argyll who became wellnigh an independent king of the 'South Isles' (from Ardnamurchan round to Bute), swaying his naval alliance between the rival powers of Scotland and Norway. In 1135 he helped David I expel the Norse from Arran and Bute, and eventually fell at Renfrew in 1164 when himself invading against Malcolm IV. Of his three sons by a daughter of Olaf, Norse king of the Isle of Man, the eldest founded the MacDougall clan of Lorne, and the next son, Reginald or Ranald, was ancestor to all the clans that derive name from his eldest son, Donald. The descendants of Donald's eldest son, Angus Mor mac Donald, formed Clan Donald South, centred on Islay. Those of the second son, Roderick or Rorie, were granted the isles north of Ardnamurchan after Haakon's defeat at Largs (Map F7) and the confinement after 1266 of the Norse to Orkney and Shetland only.

MacDonald allegiance to the Scottish crown was now unquestionable — so far as it could be induced or enforced. Bruce at Bannockburn granted the clan their jealously upheld honour of position on the right of the Scottish battle array; and in the following reign Angus Mor's grandson, John of Islay, reunited the North and South Isles by marrying the MacRorie heiress, and first assumed the Lordship of the Isles that needed royal suppression in 1493. The curbing royal policy likewise directed partitions into the separate branch-clans that follow. After 1493 the vast power of the Lords of the Isles was transferred to the Earls of Argyll in the South Isles and Huntly in the North Isles and Highlands, not without flaring resistances and memories that still cling. Chiefship shifted to the Sleat branch in Skye, called MacDonalds of the Isles to distinguish them from the branch-clans.

The numerous sept names have most various origins. Donaldson, MacConnell, Daniels, etc., are just variations from MacDonald. MacGorrie and MacHutcheon, otherwise MacQuistan, are examples of branches from chiefs Godfrey and Hugh. Small clans or families sought or fell under the MacDonald protection, or like the Macbeths took high service with the chiefs. Sometimes they took the MacDonald name irrespective of any descent from Somerled, sometimes retained their own or acquired new ones, like MacGowan (the smith's son) and Galt or Gaul (the stranger). Then when the refractory Clan Donald South was supposedly expelled from Kintyre and Islay, a strange crop of new names blossomed as in similar circumstances with the MacGregors and Lamonts.

Apart from the various strands of the MacDonald family mentioned below, two of the septs of the mighty Clan Donald, Darroch and MacSporran, have more recently been recognised by Lord Lyon King of Arms as separate, if small, clans in their own right.

## Septs:

ALASTAIR
ALLISTER
ANDERSON
BALLACH
BALLOCH
BEATH
BEATON
BETHUNE
BOWIE
BRODIE
BUDGE
BUIE
BULLOCH
CAMBRIDGE
CATHAL
CATHIL
COCHRAN
COCHRANE
COLL
COLSON
CONN
CONNAL
CONNELL
COOK
COOKE
COULL
COULSON
CRIRIE
CROMB
CROMBIE
CROOM
CRUM
DANIEL
DANIELS
DARRACH
DARROCH
DONALD
DONALDSON
DONNELL
DRAIN
DUNNEL
FORREST
FORRESTER
GALBRAITH
GALBREATH
GALL
GALT
GAULD
GAUL
GAULT
GILBRIDE
GILL
GORRIE

GORRY
GOWAN
GOWANS
HAWTHORN
HERON
HEWISON
HOUSTOUN
HOUSTON
HOWAT
HOWE
HOWIE
HOWISON
HUDSON
HUTCHEON
HUTCHESON
HUTCHIN
HUTCHINSON
HUTCHISON
HUTCHON
HUTSON
ISLES
JEFFREY
KEEGAN
KEIGHREN
KELLY
KINNELL
LAING
LANG
LEITCH
MACARTHUR
MACBEATH
MACBETH
MACBHEATH
MACBRAYNE
MACBRIDE
MACBRYDE
MACCAA
MACCAIRN
MACCAMBRIDGE
MACCARRON
MACCAW
MACCAY
MACCLUSKIE
MACCODRUM
MACCOLL
MACCONNAL
MACCONNELL
MACCOOISH
MACCOOK
MACCOSHAM
MACCRAIN
MACCRAN
MACCRIRIE

MACCRORIE
MACCRUM
MACCUAIG
MACCUISH
MACCUITHEIN
MACCUTCHEN
MACCUTCHEON
MACDANIELL
MACDRAIN
MACEACHERN
MACEACHRAN
MACELFRISH
MACELHERAN
MACGAA
MACGAW
MACGEACHY
MACGECHIE
MACGEE
MACGHEE
MACGHIE
MACGILL
MACGORRIE
MACGORRY
MACGOUN
MACGOW
MACGOWAN
MACGOWN
MACGRAIN
MACHUGH
MACHUTCHEN
MACHUTCHEON
MACILLRICK
MACILREACH
MACILREVIE
MACILRIACH
MACILWRAITH
MACILWRICK
MACKAY
MACKEACHIE
MACKEE
MACKEITHAN
MACKELLAIG
MACKELLOCH
MACKERRON
MACKEY
MACKIE
MACKIGGAN
MACKINNELL
MACLAIRISH
MACLARDY
MACLARTY
MACLAVERTY
MACLEVERTY

MACMURCHIE
MACMURCHY
MACMURDO
MACMURDOCH
MACO'SHANNAIG
MACQUILKAN
MACQUISTAN
MACQUISTEN
MACRAITH
MACREARIE
MACRORIE
MACRORY
MACRUER
MACRURY
MACRYRIE
MACSORLEY
MACSPORRAN
MACSWAN
MACSWEEN
MACWHAN
MACWHANNELL
MARK
MARQUIS
MARTIN
MAY
MURCHIE
MURCHISON
MURDOCH
MURDOSON
MURPHY
O'MAY
PATON
PATTEN
PEDEN
PURCELL
REOCH
REVIE
RIACH
RODERICK
RORIE
RORISON
RYRIE
SHANNON
SHENNAN
SORLEY
SORLIE
SPORRAN
TRAIN
WHANNEL
WHEELAN
WHELLAN
WILKIE
WILKINSON

**MACDONALD** of **Ardnamurchan**          The MacDonalds or MacIans of Ardnamurchan were founded there, in Robert Bruce's time, by Ian, a son of Angus Mor mac Donald above mentioned. In 1495 they were hosts at Mingary to James IV and assisted him against rebellious chiefs. But early in the 17th century they suffered persecution with the rest of Clan Donald South, and a number of the clan having been goaded into an act of piracy, this was unjustly remembered against their innocent Glencoe namesakes in 1692. The following are all variations from the clan name MacIan:

**Septs:**

| | | | |
|---|---|---|---|
| JOHNSON | KEENE | MACKAIN | MACKEAN |
| JOHNSTONE | MACIAN | MACKANE | MACKEAND |
| KEAN | | | |

**MACDONALD** of **Clanranald**          Strictly, all the MacDonald clans are of Clan Ranald and were frequently so termed, from Donald's father, Reginald or Ranald. Thus some confusion arises when a particular branch-clan adopts that general name, instead of their more correct form MacRanald. They derive from another Ranald, doubly descended from the first, being a younger son of John, first Lord of the Isles, by the MacRorie heiress whom he afterwards unjustly divorced. The elder son, Godfrey, claimed the North Isles inheritance in his own right, but was rejected in favour of Ranald who, being agreeable to his father's dubious superiority, was presented with the North Isles along with a thriving nest of feuds for his descendants. The clan established their position in the island-chain Benbecula to Eigg, also in their other grant from John, that rugged mainland tract from Moidart to Knoydart that Prince Charlie came to know so intimately among the faithful Clanranald.

**Septs:**

| | | | |
|---|---|---|---|
| ALCOCK | KETCHEN | MACEACHAN | MACKESSICK |
| ALISON | KETCHIN | MACEACHEN | MACKICHAN |
| ALLAN | MACACHIN | MACEACHIN | MACKISSOCK |
| ALLANSON | MACAICHAN | MACGACHAN | MACMURRAY |
| ALLEN | MACALLAN | MACGEACHAN | MACMURRICH |
| CALLAN | MACBURIE | MACISAAC | MACVARISH |
| CALLEN | MACCRINDLE | MACKEACHAN | MACVURICH |
| CURRIE | MACCURRACH | MACKECHNIE | MACVURIE |
| ISAAC | MACCURRIE | MACKEOCHAN | MACVURRICH |
| ISAACS | MACDONALD | MACKESSACK | PARK |

**MACDONALD** of **Glencoe**          This small branch-clan descends from Ian Og, i.e. 'young John', grandson of Angus Mor (see MacDonald) and step-brother to the first Lord of the Isles who, in the 14th century, settled Ian on the land having that rugged defile Glencoe, traditional birthplace of a Gaelic Homer, Ossian. These MacIans or MacDonalds lived there peaceably until the notorious 1692 massacre, when governmental spite against all sympathisers with the deposed Stewarts was vented so cold-bloodedly against a clan innocent of other offence.

**Septs:**

| | | | |
|---|---|---|---|
| HENDERSON | KEAN | MACHENDRY | MACPHILIP |
| HENDRIE | KEENE | MACHENRY | PHILIP |
| HENDRY | MACDONALD | MACIAN | PHILP |
| HENRY | MACGILP | MACKEAN | |
| JOHNSON | MACHENDRIE | MACKILLOP | |

## MACDONELL of Glengarry

The different spelling of MacDonald was adopted in the 17th century by this early division from the Clanranald branch. The Glengarry founder was Alister, second son of Donald, eldest son of the 14th-century Ranald. Apart from disputes of their own with the neighbouring MacKenzies, the Glengarries went along with the other Clanranalds, particularly in support of all the Stewart causes.

**Septs:**

| | | | |
|---|---|---|---|
| ALASTAIR | COWAN | MACOWAN | SANDERSON |
| ALEXANDER | MACCOWAN | SANDER | SAUNDERS |
| ALLISTER | MACDONELL | SANDERS | |

## MACDONNELL of Keppoch

The MacDonalds or MacDonnells of Keppoch (the spelling altered also in the 17th century) descended from Alister Currach, third son of John, first Lord of the Isles (see MacDonald) by his second wife, a sister of King Robert II. From Alister's great-grandson, Ranald, the clan was also sometimes known as Clanranald of Lochaber. For centuries they occupied their territory by unwritten clan right, despite a feudal charter granted to the Macintoshes. In their support of the Stewarts, Ian Lom, celebrated also as a Gaelic bard, acted guide for Montrose's master-stroke, the surprise march on snowbound Inverlochy Castle in 1645. And in 'the forty-five' the Keppochs captured two government companies before Prince Charlie's banner was actually raised.

**Septs:**

| | | | |
|---|---|---|---|
| MACDONELL | MACPHILIP | MICHIE | PHILP |
| MACGILLIVANTIC | MACRONALD | MICHIESON | RAINNIE |
| MACGILP | MECHIE | PHILIP | RENNIE |
| MACGLASRICH | MEEKISON | PHILIPSON | RONALD |
| MACKILLOP | MEKIE | PHILLIP | RONALDSON |
| MACMICHIE | MICHAEL | PHILLIPS | |

## MACDOUGALL

The MacDougalls of the Argyllshire district of Lorne trace back to the same ancestors as the MacDonalds, being named from the first Lord of Lorne, Dougall, the eldest son of Somerled by Ragnhildis, daughter of Olaf, the King of Man. But her mother, Africa, was already a McDougall or McDowall of the still older Galloway branch, Africa's father being Fergus Mac Dubh Gael, the powerful 12th-century Lord of Galloway and founder of several abbeys in that ancient Pictish-Celtic territory.

MacDougall history is mainly coloured by their feud with Robert Bruce after his hasty slaying of the Red Comyn, claimant to the Scottish throne (see Clan Cumming). Alexander, fourth Lord of Lorne, had married Comyn's sister. After Bruce's defeat at Methven by the English, he took for a time to the Grampians. At Dalree in Strathfillan his party was set upon by a strong force of MacDougalls, and Bruce himself escaped only by leaving his plaid grasped by a dying MacDougall. Attached to it was the magnificent Celtic 'Brooch of Lorne', still in the treasured possession of the clan chief at Dunollie. Eventually Bruce overcame both the English and the MacDougalls, the latter being restored to their Lorne lands only when Alexander's grandson, Ewen, married a niece of David II. By Ewen having only heiresses, the lordship of Lorne passed to Stewart hands, whilst the male branch of Dunollie retained the clan chiefship.

**Septs:**

| | | | |
|---|---|---|---|
| CARMICHAEL | DOUGAL | DUGALD | LIVINGSTONE |
| COLES | DOUGALL | EUNSON | LUCAS |
| CONACHER | DOWALL | HOWELL | MACCLINTOCK |
| COWAN | DOWELL | HOWELLS | MACCONACHER |
| COWEN | DUGAL | LIVINGSTON | MACCONCHER |

| | | | |
|---|---|---|---|
| MACCOUL | MACDOOL | MACEWEN | MACLUGASH |
| MACCOWAN | MACDOUGAL | MACHALE | MACLULLICH |
| MACCOWELL | MACDOUL | MACHOWELL | MACNAMELL |
| MACCOYLE | MACDOWALL | MACKICHAN | MACOUAL |
| MACCULLAGH | MACDOWELL | MACLINDEN | MACOUL |
| MACCULLOCH | MACDUGALD | MACLINTOCK | MACOWAN |
| MACDILL | MACEWAN | MACLUCAS | MACOWEN |

## MACDUFF

Like the clan's claim of descent from Clan Alpin, the real story of Shakespeare's Macduff overthrowing Macbeth in 1056 remains uncertain, but the hereditary special privileges and dispensations once known as 'Law Clan Macduff' must have originated from some other notable service. Thus, it was accepted even by Edward I, 'Hammer of the Scots', that a Scottish king could be properly crowned only by a Macduff. Edward retained that young chief at the English court and gave him his granddaughter's hand, but Macduff's sister Isabel, Countess of Buchan, crowned King Robert Bruce in 1306. Captured later by Edward, she was punished by confinement in a cage at Berwick.

Until among the first Earls created by David I, the Macduff Thanes of Fife held their territory in the old Celtic manner 'by grace of God', not from the King — hence occasional mentions of the county as though of itself a 'kingdom'. Their direct line failed with another 14th-century Isabel, but the Duff families then first heard of in Aberdeenshire claim to carry on the clan. They reacquired a title Earl, then Duke of Fife, but their territory remained around where they founded the fishing town Macduff.

Septs:

| | | | |
|---|---|---|---|
| DUFF | FYFFE | SPENCE | WEMYSS |
| FIFE | HUME | SPENS | |
| FYFE | KILGOUR | WEEMS | |

## MACFARLANE

This clan of Loch-Lomondside and Arrochar descended from the old Celtic earls of Lennox through Gilchrist, younger brother of Malduin, a 13th-century Earl. The name derives from his great-grandson, Bartholomew or Parlan. From failures in the direct male line, the clan lands passed to other ownership by feudal law, while rightfully elective male chiefs were dispossessed. From this disorganisation and a feud with the powerful Colquhouns resulting in that Chief being slain in 1608, the clan were for a time outlawed like the MacGregors, or transferred elsewhere in Scotland or to Ireland. Many groups thereafter retained the various other names they adopted at the time, like the MacAllans in Aberdeenshire.

Septs:

| | | | |
|---|---|---|---|
| ALLAN | KENNIESON | MACKINLAY | MUNNOCK |
| ALLANACH | LEAPER | MACNAIR | NAPIER |
| ALLANSON | LEIPPER | MACNEUR | PARLAN |
| ALLEN | LENNOX | MACNIDER | PARLANE |
| ALLISON | MACAINDRA | MACNITER | ROBB |
| BARTHOLOMEW | MACALLAN | MACNUIR | SMITH |
| BARTIE | MACCAUSE | MACPARLAND | SPREULL |
| BARTLEMAN | MACCONDACH | MACPARLANE | SPROUL |
| BARTLET | MACCONDY | MACPHARLAN | STALKER |
| BARTLETT | MACERRACHER | MACROB | THOMASON |
| BARTY | MACFARLAN | MACROBB | WEAVER |
| BRYCE | MACGEOCH | MACWALTER | WEBSTER |
| CALLANDER | MACGREUSICH | MACWILLIAM | WEIR |
| CUNNISON | MACGURK | MILLAR | WILLIAMSON |
| GALBRAITH | MACINALLY | MILLER | WYLIE |
| GALBREATH | MACINSTALKER | MONACH | WYLLIE |
| GALLOWAY | MACJAMES | MUNNOCH | |

**MACFIE**     The MacFies claim to be one of the ancient Clan Alpin, and come no doubt from some dark-featured ancestor, as is signified by the earlier form MacDuffie; perhaps from the Dubhshith who in 1164 was lector at the cathedral on the sacred isle of Iona, where there is also a monument to a later McFie chief. Twenty miles south lies Colonsay, which was the clan's own island, with their burial-ground on neighbouring Oronsay. In the 17th century they were dispossessed and dispersed in various directions. The MacFie followers of Cameron of Lochiel earned particular tribute at Culloden.

**Septs:**

| | | | |
|---|---|---|---|
| CATHIE | MACCATHIE | MACGUFFIE | MACVEE |
| DUFFIE | MACCOOISH | MACHAFFIE | MACVIE |
| DUFFY | MACCUISH | MACNICOL | |
| FEE | MACDUFFIE | MACPHEE | |
| MACCAFFIE | MACFEE | MACPHIE | |

**MACGILLIVRAY**     Originally an Argyllshire clan and one of the great MacDonald group, the MacGillivrays were involved in the latter's defeat in 1222 by Alexander II. Thereafter, a branch in Morvern came under protection of the MacLeans of Mull, but about 1263 the chief section removed to Macintosh country and joined Clan Chattan under that leadership. However, at Culloden with Prince Charlie it was their chief, MacGillivray of Dunmaglass, who most gallantly led the Macintoshes. The MacInnes branch of the Morvern MacGillivrays appear as a separate clan.

**Septs:**

| | | | |
|---|---|---|---|
| GILRAY | MACGILROY | MACILROY | ROY |
| GILROY | MACGILVRA | MACILVRAE | |
| GILVRAY | MACGILVRAY | MILROY | |

**MACGREGOR**     Recorded in Glen Orchy from about the 12th century and spreading to Glenstrae and several Perthshire glens, the MacGregors take their motto *Is Rioghal mo dhream*, 'My race is Royal', from a traditional ancestor, Gregor or Girig, of the ancient Clan Alpin dynasty. They held doggedly to the old Celtic clan rule of defending possession by the sword, in defiance of 'sheepskin' feudal charters obtained through marriage or more dubious means by powerful neighbours having a closer approach to the government's ear — notably the Campbells, Grahams and Colquhouns. After a defeat by these last at Glen Fruin in 1603, there came a long succession of vindictive edicts, fomenting and taking full excuse from the MacGregors' spirit of untamed resentment. The clan was outlawed, and a ban on using their surname not lifted until 1784 except in the time of the Stewart Restoration, in recognition of their loyal service with Montrose. From these prescriptions arose the many 'sept' names then adopted by scattered groups of MacGregors — also the remarkable career of Rob Roy and Scott's stirring song 'The MacGregors' Gathering'.

**Septs:**

| | | | |
|---|---|---|---|
| ARGYL | CLARK | FISHER | GREIG |
| ARROWSMITH | COMRIE | FLETCHER | GREWAR |
| BARROWMAN | CRAIGDALLIE | GAIR | GREYSON |
| BEGLAND | CRERAR | GOODSIR | GRIER |
| BLACK | CROWTHER | GREER | GRIERSON |
| BOWER | DENNISON | GREGG | GRIGG |
| BOWMAKER | DENSON | GREGOR | GRIGOR |
| CAIRD | DOCHART | GREGORSON | GRUER |
| CALLENDAR | DOCHERTY | GREGORY | GUDGER |
| CALLUM | DOWIE | GREGSON | GUINNESS |

## Septs:

| | | | |
|---|---|---|---|
| JOHNSTON | MACDOUGAL | MACNEICE | PATTULLO |
| KING | MACEWEN | MACNEISH | PEAT |
| KIRKWOOD | MACGEACH | MACNESS | PETER |
| LAIKIE | MACGREWAR | MACNEY | PETERS |
| LECKIE | MACGRIGOR | MACNIE | PETERSON |
| LECKY | MACGROUTHER | MACNIESH | PETRIE |
| MACADAM | MACGRUDER | MACNISH | ROBINS |
| MACAINSH | MACGRUER | MACNOCAIRD | ROY |
| MACALDOWIE | MACGRUMEN | MACNUCATOR | SKINNER |
| MACALESTER | MACGRUTHER | MACONACHIE | STALKER |
| MACANGUS | MACIAN | MACPETER | STIRLING |
| MACANISH | MACILDOWIE | MACPETRIE | STRINGER |
| MACARA | MACILDUFF | MACWILLIAM | TAINSH |
| MACAREE | MACILDUY | MAGREW | TOSSACK |
| MACCAINSH | MACINNES | MALLOCH | WALKER |
| MACCANCE | MACINSTALKER | NEISH | WELIVER |
| MACCANSH | MACINTYRE | NELSON | WHITE |
| MACCONACHIE | MACLEISTER | NICE | WHYTE |
| MACCONDACH | MACLIVER | NISH | WILCOX |
| MACCONDOCHIE | MACNAY | NUCATOR | WILLOX |
| MACCROUTHER | MACNEA | ORR | |
| MACCRUITER | MACNEE | PATERSON | |

**MACINNES**     The name Innes here comes from the Gaelic pronunciation of MacAngus. A Morvern branch of the Clan MacGillivray, the MacInneses were for long Constables of the important fortress of Kinlochaline on the Sound of Mull. MacInneses are also recorded as hereditary instructors in archery to the Clan MacKinnon. The MacMasters were originally a separate clan of neighbouring Ardgour, driven from there by MacLeans in the 14th century.

Angus being an ancient and favourite Scottish forename, MacInnes and its variants sprang up independently of the above clan, as in Galloway and notably in Perthshire, where the MacNish or MacCance septs are attributed to MacGregor origin.

## Septs:

| | | |
|---|---|---|
| ANGUS | MACANISH | MACCANSH |
| MACAINSH | MACCAINSH | MACMASTER |
| MACANGUS | MACCANCE | MASTERSON |

**MACINTOSH**     This leading division of the old Clan Chattan claims the Macintoshes descended from Seach or Shaw, son of a Macduff thane of Fife. Assisting Malcolm IV about 1160 to quell a rebel rising in Moray, he was awarded lands near Inverness and the constableship of that castle. The name means 'Son of the Toisich' or 'Toshach', i.e. of the leader or general. The clan occupied an important central position but in clashes with neighbours like the ambitious Gordons managed well to maintain itself, through astute compromise between the two types of Scottish feudalism. Though in many ways adhering to the old Celtic clan system, their actual power was based on royal charters and a female inheritance. In the last of their successive rallies for the Stewarts, the clan was raised for Prince Charlie by Lady Macintosh, despite the neutrality of her husband, the Chief. Placed under command of a MacGillivray, they were the first to charge at Culloden.

The clan chief, Mackintosh of Mackintosh, retains a superfluous English 'k' in the name. The MacThomas or MacTavish septs, settled in Glenshee or West Angus, derive from a son of a 14th-century Macintosh chief, whilst the Farquharson and Shaw branches are regarded as having become separate clans. The MacThomas sept has also recently become a separate clan.

**Septs:**

| | | | |
|---|---|---|---|
| ADAMSON | HARDY | MACCOMIE | MACRITCHIE |
| AYSON | HEGGIE | MACCONCHIE | MACTAUSE |
| CASH | HIGGISON | MACFAIL | MACTAVISH |
| CLARK | HOSICK | MACFALL | MACTHOMAS |
| CLARKE | HOSSACK | MACFAULD | MACVAIL |
| CLARKSON | LEARY | MACGLASHAN | NAIRN |
| CLERK | MACANDREW | MACGLASHEN | NAIRNE |
| COMBE | MACARTNEY | MACHARDIE | NEVISON |
| COMBIE | MACAY | MACHARDY | NIVEN |
| CREARER | MACCAISH | MACKEGGIE | NOBLE |
| CRERAR | MACCARDNEY | MACKIESON | PAUL |
| DALLAS | MACCARTNEY | MACKILLICAN | RIPLEY |
| DOLES | MACCASH | MACKINTOSH | RITCHIE |
| EASON | MACCAUSE | MACLEAR | SIVEWRIGHT |
| EASSON | MACCHLERY | MACLEARY | TARRELL |
| EGGIE | MACCLAIR | MACLEHOSE | TAWESON |
| EGGO | MACCLEARY | MACLERIE | TAWSE |
| ELDER | MACCOLM | MACNEVIN | THOM |
| ESSON | MACCOMAS | MACNIVEN | THOMS |
| GLENNIE | MACCOMBE | MACOMIE | TOSH |
| GLENNY | MACCOMBICH | MACOMISH | TOSHACH |
| HARDIE | MACCOMBIE | MACPHAIL | |

**MACINTYRE** By tradition a branch from the Skye MacDonalds, the clan achieved most note from their bards and musicians. The name means 'Son of the wright' or 'carpenter'. For centuries, until 1810, inhabiting Glen Noe off Loch Etive, the MacIntyres were too small to stand alone and first followed the banner of the Appin Stewarts then latterly of the Campbell superiors of their land, though one branch became hereditary pipers to the Menzies chiefs.

**Septs:**

| | | | |
|---|---|---|---|
| MACCOSHAM | MACKINTYRE | MACTIER | TYRE |
| MACINTIRE | MACTEAR | MACTIRE | WRIGHT |

**MACKAY** Like their MacKenzie neighbours, the MacKays of the Cape Wrath district, sometimes termed Clan Morgan after a 14th-century chief, may have been one of the tribes of Moray expelled from there for revolts in the 12th century. This powerful clan came often into dispute with others, not excluding the great Lords of the Isles. A strong section of the clan became established under these lords in Argyll and Galloway, and the name MacKay derives from Morgan's grandson Aodh, whose mother was a MacNeil of Gigha. MacKays or MacAys of Clan Chattan, from Inverness-shire eastward, are really of Clan MacDhai, i.e., Davidsons.

Clan MacKay devoted much zeal to the Protestant Reformation. Two thousand of them crossed the North Sea to serve that cause in the Thirty-Years' War. Charles I raised their Chief to Lord Dreay, yet their grandsons' religious mistrust of the Stewarts made them one of the anti-Jacobite clans.

**Septs:**

| | | | |
|---|---|---|---|
| ALLAN | MACALLAN | MACGAA | MACKEE |
| BAIN | MACBAIN | MACGAW | MACKIE |
| BAYNE | MACCAA | MACGEE | MACPHAIL |
| KAY | MACCAW | MACGHEE | MACQUE |
| KEY | MACCAY | MACGHIE | MACQUEY |

**Septs:**

| | | | |
|---|---|---|---|
| MACQUOID | MORGAN | POLE | SCOBIE |
| MACVAIL | NEILSON | POLESON | WILLIAMSON |
| MACVAIN | NELSON | POLSON | |
| MACVANE | PAUL | REAY | |

## MACKENZIE

Perhaps, like the MacKays and MacLeans, one of the old transplanted tribes from Moray, though firmly rooted in Ross-shire ever since, this clan took their name, MacKenny or MacKenzie, after a 13th-century chief Kenneth, descended from Colin of the Aird who was ancestor also to the Celtic Earls of Ross. When that earldom fell by marriage to the Lord of the Isles, the clan followed the MacDonald lead until these lords were suppressed. Independence attained, the MacKenzies became by the 17th century the most powerful clan of the West after the Campbells, and their chief, MacKenzie of Kintail, was raised to Lord Seaforth by James VI. This earldom was forfeited through the clans sharing the Jacobite ventures but restored in 1778 when the Seaforth Highlanders regiment was founded.

**Septs:**

| | | | |
|---|---|---|---|
| CHARLES | KENNETH | MACKENNA | MACVINISH |
| CHARLESON | KENNETHSON | MACKENNEY | MACVINNIE |
| CLUNESS | KYNOCH | MACKERLICH | MACWEENY |
| CLUNIES | MACAWEENEY | MACKINNEY | MACWHINNIE |
| CROMARTY | MACBEOLAIN | MACMURCHIE | MURCHIE |
| IVERACH | MACCONNACH | MACMURCHY | MURCHISON |
| IVERSON | MACIVER | MACQUEENIE | SMART |
| IVORY | MACIVOR | MACVANISH | |

## MACKINNON

By old tradition the MacKinnons claim to be of the royal Clan Alpin stock, descended and named from Fingon, brother to Andrew who was ancestor to Grigor and the MacGregors. From actual records we find them from about 1400 established as vassals of the Lords of the Isles in East Skye, including Castles Strathardle and Maol, and in Mull, with branches from Tiree to Arran. Like the other Alpin branch MacFie, they had at least a professional interest in the holy isle of Iona, where several MacFingons or MacKinnons were abbots around the 15th century.

The clan 'came out' with Montrose and in both Jacobite rebellions. In July 1746 the aged Chief and his family took over from Flora MacDonald a further anxious stage in aiding Prince Charlie's escape after Culloden.

**Septs:**

| | | | |
|---|---|---|---|
| LOVE | MACKINNING | MACMORRAN | SHERRIE |
| MACINNON | MACKINVEN | MACSHERRIE | SHERRY |

## MACLACHLAN

From time immemorial the clan home has been Strathlachlan on the Cowal side of Loch Fyne, beside their neighbours, the MacEwens and Lamonts. Ancient tradition has it the three were originally founded by brothers, and these related by marraige, if not descent, to the ancient Kings of Ireland and Somerled Lords of the Isles. Their name may derive from that founder Lachlan, or from the O Loughlins, or from a later chief, Lachlan Mor of the 13th century. A section of the clan acquired Loch Awe territory under Campbell leadership, and another similarly served with the Lochiel Camerons.

The MacEwan group of septs might fairly claim separate clanship; whilst those of them in Lorne and Breadalbane are attributed to a MacDougall origin.

**Septs:**

| | | | |
|---|---|---|---|
| EUNSON | EWEN | EWING | LACHIE |
| EWAN | EWENSON | GILCHRIST | LACHLAN |

**Septs:**

| | | | |
|---|---|---|---|
| LAUCHLAN | MACEWEN | MACKEWAN | MACLAGHLAN |
| MACCUNE | MACGILCHRIST | MACKEWN | MACLAUCHLAN |
| MACOUNN | MACKEON | MACKUEN | MACLAUGHLIN |
| MACEWAN | MACKEOWN | MACKUNE | |

**MACLAINE of Lochbuie**  See MACLEAN.

**MACLAREN**  The older form MacLaurin is nearer to the Gaelic pronunciation. Whether originally called after the martyred St Lawrence, or from Loarn, son of the Erc who founded Scottish Dalriada about 503, and namer of the district of Lorne, the clan does claim descent from three brothers from the area now Argyll, who served with Kenneth MacAlpin in his successful campaign of 843-50 to unite the Northern Picts into Scotland. A branch remained in their first home-country and was for long in possession of Tiree, but those three brothers' awards in Balquhidder and Strathearn became the clan's main territory. Here they enter records surviving from the 13th century, and at Balquhidder lies Rob Roy MacGregor in the MacLaurin burial-ground: not the only old encroachment between these two clans. In their long record of loyalty the MacLaurins frequently followed the Appin Stewarts, with whom they had blood ties, and it was a MacLaurin who escaped Cumberland's troops by flinging himself over the Moffat 'Beef-tub'.

**Septs:**

| | | | |
|---|---|---|---|
| FAED | LOWSON | MACLAURIN | PATTERSON |
| LARNACH | MACFADE | MACPATRICK | PETERKIN |
| LAURENCE | MACCLARENCE | MACPETRIE | PETERS |
| LAURENSON | MACCRORIE | MACPHAIT | PETERSON |
| LAW | MACFAIT | MACPHATER | RORIE |
| LAWRENCE | MACFATER | MACRORIE | RORISON |
| LAWSON | MACFEAD | MACRORY | |
| LOW | MACFEAT | PATERSON | |
| LOWE | MACGRORY | PATRICK | |

**MACLEAN**  Though the name means 'Son of a devotee of St John', MacLeans claim as legendary ancestor a 5th-century Gillean-na Tuaidhe, i.e. Gillean of the Battle-axe. They may have been transplanted by Malcolm IV from Glen Urquhart, as one of the Celtic tribes then rebelling against centralised feudalism. A century later, the 13th, we find them in Mull, strongly established as vassals of Clan Donald, and soon one of the most powerful clans behind the Lords of the Isles, as at Harlaw 1411 and until these lords' suppression in 1493 and an ensuing feud with the MacDonalds that lasted till 1498. Their territory ranged from Coll and Tiree to Ardgour on the mainland, though the main families remained MacLeans of Duart (Chief) and Maclaines of Lochbuie, both in Mull. Their Chief fell protecting James IV at Flodden, and with their maxim the MacLeans must never turn their backs to a foe, the clan were prominent in all the Stewart causes.

**Septs:**

| | | | |
|---|---|---|---|
| BEATH | MACBAY | MACFETRIDGE | MACVAY |
| BEATON | MACBEATH | MACGILLIVRAY | MACVEAGH |
| BEY | MACBETH | MACGILVRA | MACVEY |
| BLACK | MACBEY | MACILDOWIE | PADON |
| GILLAN | MACBHEATH | MACILDUFF | PATON |
| GILLAND | MACCLANE | MACILDUY | PATTEN |
| GILLIAN | MACCLEAN | MACILVORA | PATTON |
| GILLON | MACCORMICK | MACLAINE | PEDEN |
| GILZEAN | MACFADYEN | MACLERGAN | RANKEN |
| HUIE | MACFADZEAN | MACPHADDEN | RANKINE |
| LEAN | MACFAYDEN | MACRANKIN | |

## MACLENNAN

**MACLENNAN**  The small MacLennan clan of Kintail originated from a southern Logan marrying a Fraser and forming a Logan clan, at first in Easter Ross. Their 13th-century chief, Gilliegorm, then falling into strife with the Frasers, was killed and his widow imprisoned. Her posthumous son was deformed, whether by nature or by the gaolers, and delivered to the Beauly monks for a priestly education. He did found churches at Kilmor in Skye and Kilchrennan in Glenelg, but he also carried his clan, along with the closely associated Macraes, across to Kintail on the west coast, where he married and named his son Gille Fhinnan, after the Celtic St Finnan. From MacGill'innan comes 'MacLennan'. Sections of the clan later attached themselves to the Frasers and MacKenzies.

**Septs:**

| LOBBAN | LOGAN |
|--------|-------|

**MACLEOD of Harris**  The MacLeod chiefs claim descent from Leod, nephew of Magnus, the 13th-century last of the Norse kings of the Isle of Man; and from Leod's two sons, Tormod and Torquil, come respectively the Harris and Lewis branches. The bulk of the clan, however, remains of native Celtic stock. Tormod's grandson Malcolm was awarded a charter of Glenelg territory by David II and by marriage acquired the clan's large foothold in Skye, with its famed fortress of Dunvegan as the Chief's seat. Harris was held by MacLeods as vassals to Clan Donald until the Lords of the Isles were forfeited. Thereafter, clear of that entanglement, they aided the MacLeans against the MacDonalds. At Worcester in 1651, the clan lost so many men for Charles II that the other clans agreed to exonerate them from further conflicts.

**Septs:**

| BEATON | HARROLD | MACCUAIG | NORMAN |
|--------|---------|----------|--------|
| BETHUNE | MACANDIE | MACHAROLD | NORMAND |
| BETON | MACCAIG | MACLURE | WILLIAMSON |
| GRIMMOND | MACCLURE | MACRAILD | |
| HAROLD | MACCRIMMON | MACWILLIAM | |

**MACLEOD of Lewis**  The clan of Torquil (see above) early became so powerful as to dispute the superiority of the Harris branch chiefship, attaining at least an independent status. Important branches were the MacGillechallum or MacLeods of Raasay, and those of Assynt. The MacNicols (Nicolson etc.) were originally an independent clan of the Assynt district. They moved to the Portree corner of Skye after a 14th-century Lewis MacLeod had married their Chief's heiress.

**Septs:**

| ASKEY | MACASKILL | MACCORQUODALE | NICHOLSON |
|-------|-----------|---------------|-----------|
| AULAY | MACCABE | MACGILLECHALLUM | NICOL |
| CALLAM | MACAULAY | MACKASKILL | NICOLL |
| CALLUM | MACCALLUM | MACLEWIS | NICOLSON |
| CASKEY | MACCASKIE | MACNICHOL | NORIE |
| CASKIE | MACCASKILL | MACNICOL | NORRIE |
| LEWIS | MACCORKILL | MACNICOLL | TOLMIE |
| MACALLUM | MACCORKINDALE | MALCOLMSON | |
| MACASKIE | MACCORKLE | NICHOLL | |

**MACMILLAN**  Believed to be of descent from Methlan, son of a 13th-century Buchanan chief, MacMillans became known about then around Loch Arkaig, with a branch by Loch Tay. From here in the 16th century their chief possession became Knapdale through marriage with a MacNeill heiress; and in Galloway also a branch developed who were later to achieve note as Covenanters.

At first dependent on the Lords of the Isles, the MacMillans afterwards lost their clan lands to bigger neighbours, the Lochaber group becoming fighting followers of the Camerons, whilst some from Knapdale avoided Campbell 'protection' by migrating to Arran. The Baxter sept claim descent from a Chief's son who once eluded pursuit by assuming the guise of a busy baker.

**Septs:**

| | | | |
|---|---|---|---|
| BAXTER | BLUE | BROWN | MACNAMELL |
| BELL | BROUN | MACBAXTER | |

## MACNAB

The MacNabs are of ancient origin in Breadalbane and claim to be descended of Clan Alpin, also from a family of hereditary abbots of St Fillan's monastery once in Glendochart, hence *Mac an Aba*, 'Son of the abbot'. The old Celtic church did not stipulate celibacy. The Dewar sept long held custody of the beautiful Celtic 'Crozier of St Fillan', now in the Royal Museum of Scotland, Edinburgh. The Gaelic form of St Fillan is the origin of several sept names including Cleland and MacLellan for whom separate clanship has been claimed.

From their once extensive clan lands there remains only the MacNab burial island at Killin. The reduction arose through supporting MacDougalls against the unforgetting Bruce; and again for following Montrose, when their royalist Chief was taken prisoner and escaped only to fall at Worcester 1651 with many other Highlanders. A later kenspeckle Chief was the subject of Raeburn's jaunty portrait *The MacNab*.

**Septs:**

| | | | |
|---|---|---|---|
| ABBOT | CLELLAND | GILLAND | MACCLELLAND |
| ABBOTSON | DEWAR | GILLILAND | MACNABB |
| ABBOTT | GILFILLAN | MACCLELLAND | MACNAIR |
| CLELAND | GILLAN | MACLELLAN | |

## MACNAUGHTON

With the ancient name Nechtan, borne by four Pictish kings, the MacNaughtons claim as progenitor a chief of one of the powerful Moray tribes transplanted by Malcolm IV. This Nachtan Mor and his clan he settled in Strathtay and Strathspey, but within a century we find them migrating again to greater power in Argyll, with charters to their chief seat at Dunderave on Loch Fyne and another stronghold, Fraoch Eilean, in Loch Awe. Other fortresses of Dun Nachtan in Lewis and Strathspey recall their wide-ranged influence. This became severely reduced from the clan's joining the various Stewart risings.

**Septs:**

| | | | |
|---|---|---|---|
| HENDERSON | MACHENDRY | MACNAUCHTON | MACQUAKER |
| HENDRIE | MACHENRY | MACNAUGHT | MACVICAR |
| HENDRY | MACKENDRICK | MACNAUGHTAN | NEVIN |
| HENRY | MACKENRICK | MACNAYER | NEVISON |
| KENDRICK | MACKNIGHT | MACNEUR | NIVEN |
| KENRICK | MACMATH | MACNEVIN | NIVISON |
| MACBRAYNE | MACNACHTAN | MACNIVEN | PORTER |
| MACCRACKEN | MACNAGHTEN | MACNUIR | WEIR |
| MACHENDRIE | MACNAIR | MACNUYER | |

## MACNEIL

Niall, Nigel or Neil, the clan's founder in Bruce's reign, had lands in Knapdale and Kintyre and was probably of Clan Donald stock. MacNeills in Galloway at least as early as Bruce may be of the ancient Irish O'Neills. The MacNeil clan at first followed the Lords of the Isles, then after 1493 the two separated braches of Barra and Gigha took opposite sides with the MacLeans and Islay MacDonalds respectively. Neil's great-grandson was in 1427 granted Barra, the Hebridean isle with its forbidding islet-castle

Kisimul, and South Uist. Torquil MacNeill, about the same time, founded the branch-clan of Gigha, also of Taynish and Colonsay.

The clan's maritime tradition appears in *The Highland Fair*, Mitchell's ballad-opera of 1731, when the Bardess omits Noah from one long genealogy: 'The MacNeil had a boat of its own!' And one of the clan was chief designer of the Cunarders *Queen Mary* and *Queen Elizabeth*.

**Septs:**

| | | | |
|---|---|---|---|
| MACGOUGAN | MACNEALE | NEAL | NELSON |
| MACGRAIL | MACNEILAGE | NEALE | NIEL |
| MACGUGAN | MACNEILL | NEIL | NIELSON |
| MACGUIGAN | MACNELLY | NEILL | |
| MACNEAL | MACNIEL | NEILSON | |

**MACPHERSON**         The name means 'Son of the Parson', one Murriach or Murdoch who in 1153 succeeded to the Chiefship of Clan Chattan (see thereunder) and obtained special dispensation to marry. His third son evinced a skill that established one source of the numerous Smith families. Previously of Lochaber, the MacPhersons were settled in Badenoch by Robert Bruce on land they had wrested from his Comyn rivals. A great quarrel with the Davidsons was settled by winning that 1396 combat of the North Inch of Perth, with the help of Hal Gow o' the Wynd — also doubtless by playing the clan's Fairy Chanter.

After Culloden, Cluny MacPherson shared his Benalder 'Cage' for weeks with Prince Charlie and remained himself in hiding for nine years. Despite large rewards offered, the loyal clansmen betrayed neither. James MacPherson (1738-96), with his version of Ossian's epic that first directed world attention to Celtic legends, instigated a new era of 'Romantic' taste.

**Septs:**

| | | | |
|---|---|---|---|
| ARCHIBALD | GILLESPIE | MACCLEISH | MACLERIE |
| CATTANACH | GILLIE | MACCURRACH | MACLISE |
| CLARK | GILLIES | MACCURRIE | MACLISH |
| CLARKE | GOUDIE | MACGILLIES | MACMURDO |
| CLARKSON | GOW | MACGOUN | MACMURDOCH |
| CLERK | GOWAN | MACGOW | MACMURRICH |
| CLUNIE | GOWANS | MACGOWAN | MACVURICH |
| CLUNY | LEARY | MACKEITH | MACVURRICH |
| CURRIE | LEES | MACLEAR | MURDOCH |
| ELLIS | MACCHLERY | MACLEARY | MURDOSON |
| ELLISON | MACCLAIR | MACLEES | PEARSON |
| FERSEN | MACCLEARY | MACLEISH | SMITH |

**MACQUARRIE**         The name is from Guarie or Godfrey, and the MacQuarries claim Clan Alpin descent from his being a brother to the Fingon, reputed founder of the Clan MacKinnon. Settled since at least the 13th century in the Isle of Ulva and the neighbouring part of Mull, until 1493 the clan followed the Lords of the Isles, thereafter the MacLeans of Duart. The last Chief joined the army aged 63, dying aged 103 in 1818. The name is prominent on Australian maps, from a clansman who was long Governor of New South Wales. An earlier one founded the Irish MacGuires.

**Septs:**

| | | | |
|---|---|---|---|
| MACCORRIE | MACGORRIE | MACQUAIRE | MACQUIRE |
| MACCORRY | MACGUARIE | MACQUARIE | QUARRY |
| MACGORRY | MACGUIRE | MACQUHIRR | WHARRIE |

**MACQUEEN**        Originally of Skye as a small sept of the great MacDonalds, the Clan Macqueen or MacSweyn derives from some ancestor of the Norse name Sweyn. The Castle and Loch Sween in Knapdale were named from a 13th-century branch which later became absorbed by MacMillans and Lamonts. The chief branch, or Clan Revan, migrated via Moidart to Strathdearn by the River Findhorn. Here, with their chief Revan MacMulmor MacSweyn, they settled about 1410 as a contingent of Clan Chattan under Macintosh leadership. Some Irish forms of the name are of non-Norse origin, and if meaning 'son of Conn' may again relate them to the legendary Celtic ancestor of Clan Donald.

| Septs: | | | |
|---|---|---|---|
| | MACSWAIN | MACSWEEN | REVANS |
| | MACSWAN | MACWHAN | SWAN |

**MACRAE**        The Clan Macrae are first heard of settled at Clunes, near Beauly. In the 14th century, through quarrels with the Frasers of that locality, they accompanied their neighbours the MacLennans across Ross-shire to Kintail. Settled in the mountain-encircled Glenshiel, the Macraes commanded Loch Alsh from the fortress of Eilean Donan, restored by a 20th-century Chief, still its hereditary Constable. The name belongs to a small class of 'Macs' not meaning the son of some ancestor. The earliest form, Macrath, was a baptismal term, translated as 'Son of grace', or 'of good-fortune'. Other names for the clan have been 'the Wild Macraes' and, from long adherence with the MacKenzies, 'Seaforth's Mail-shirt'.

**Septs:**

| | | | |
|---|---|---|---|
| CRAE | MACCRAW | MACGRATH | MACRAY |
| CREE | MACCRAY | MACGRAW | MACRIE |
| MACARA | MACCREA | MACHRAY | RAE |
| MACARRA | MACCREATH | MACRA | RAITH |
| MACCRA | MACCREE | MACRACH | RAY |
| MACCRACH | MACCRIE | MACRAITH | REA |
| MACCRAE | MACCROW | MACRATH | REATH |
| MACCRAITH | MACCROY | MACRAW | |

**MACTHOMAS**        Founded by Thomas, a natural son of Angus, sixth Chief of Clan Macintosh in the 14th century. A clan MacThomas appears in a list of Clans belonging to the Ancient Federation of Clan Chattan. In a later role (1587) there occurs 'Clan MacThomas in Glenshee'.

**Septs:**

| | | | |
|---|---|---|---|
| McCOMAS | MACCOMIE | TAMSON | THOMASON |
| McCOMB | McHAMISH | THOM | THOMS |
| MACCOMBIE | MACTHOMAS | THOMAS | THOMSON |

**MALCOLM**        The name means a Devotee of St Columba, the founder of Iona and missionary to the Northern Picts. Borne by four Scottish kings, it early became a favourite Christian name and then surname in various parts of Scotland. One family of Malcolms had charters of Stirlingshire lands from the 14th century.

The Highland clan is by tradition a branch of the MacGillechallums, otherwise MacLeods of Raasay. From the early 15th century they became established in the Loch Awe district under Campbell leadership.

| Septs: | | | |
|---|---|---|---|
| | CALLAM | MACALLUM | MALCOLM |
| | CALLUM | MACCALLUM | |

**MATHESON** The Celtic clan MacMaghan or MacMathan, otherwise Clan of the Bear, once held a powerful position in Wester Ross. Tradition claims they assisted Kenneth MacAlpin in 843 against the Picts, also that the old Earls of Ross and the Clan MacKenzie came from their stock. They were Constables of Eilean Donan Castle before the Macraes. From feuds with neighbours they became much reduced and dispersed, and from the 15th century followed the MacKenzie banner. Confusion arises from their adopting, about that time, the somewhat similar south-country name Matheson, really Matthew-son, itself an old name in Scotland under various forms.

Septs:

| | | | |
|---|---|---|---|
| BAIRNSON | MACMAHON | MASSIE | MATHIESON |
| MACBIRNIE | MACMATH | MATTHEWSON | |
| MACBURNIE | MASSEY | MATHIE | |

**MAXWELL** The name is from lands called after Maccus'-well, a fishing-reach of the River Tweed by Kelso. The Border clan might have derived from Maccus, a 10th-century king of Man and the Isles, but more likely from some Norman family settled there by Malcolm Canmore and destined to hold many high offices thereafter. From being Sheriffs of Teviotdale, their chief territory became Nithsdale from the 13th century and the Solway castle of Caerlaverock their headquarters. Frequently Wardens of the West March, they were fully engaged in the border struggles, and the fourth Lord Maxwell fell at Flodden. Among their more private feuds, the Johnstons were their chief adversaries. James Clerk Maxwell in 1865 first explained the feasability of radio transmission.

**MENZIES** The 'z' comes from erroneous copying of the old written 'y', and even without that, the pronunciation has varied considerably, from *Meinn* in the Gaelic to 'Men-yes', 'Ming-us', etc. The Perthshire clan took its name from the de Meyners (in England becoming Manners), one of the many Norman families installed around the 12th century to organise the people, whether for peace or war. Without being missing from Bannockburn or Prince Charlie's ranks and events between, the Menzies earned their chief repute constructively. 'The fat herds of the Menzies' were well quoted by other clans, whilst the Araucarian Pine ('Monkey puzzle') and more usefully widespread larch were each introduced to Scotland by a Menzies about two centuries ago. The clan itself spread widely. From Atholl and Breadalbane offshoots reached Nithsdale, Lanarkshire, Kippen, Aberdeenshire and Fife.

Septs:

| | | | |
|---|---|---|---|
| DEWAR | MACMINN | MEIN | MINNUS |
| MACINDEOR | MACMONIES | MEINE | |
| MACMENZIES | MEANIES | MENGUES | |
| MACMIN | MEANS | MINN | |

**MORRISON** The Morrisons shared Lewis in the Hebrides with their earliest neighbours the MacLeods and the MacAulays. They took their name from a chief Maurice, after being earlier known as MacGilmore from some 'son of a devotee of Mary', but the change occurred before the Reformation. For a period ending with the MacKenzies taking charge of Lewis in 1613, Morrisons held the strenuous post of hereditary Brieve, or arbitrating judge, in the 'Long Isle', though in face of the powerful MacLeods this was a source rather of feud than of justice. Branches of the clan became settled in Harris, Skye, the Northwest mainland, and Aberdeenshire. A Perthshire group claim as its ancestor the Buchanan Clan's Maurice.

Septs:

| | | |
|---|---|---|
| BRIEVE | GILMOUR | MACBRIEVE |
| GILMORE | JUDGE | MORISON |

**MUNRO**          Tradition gives the Munros an Irish origin, from the river Roe in Derry, but for about eight centuries now their Chiefs have been Munro of Foulis, on the Cromarty Firth, established there as vassals of the Earls of Ross until that overlordship was removed in 1476. They were with Bruce at Bannockburn. Although friendly to Mary Queen of Scots, Munros became ardent Protestants, like the MacKays, and acquired army distinction with Gustavus Adolphus in Sweden and at home on behalf of governments clearly of their own religious persuasion.

James Monroe, fifth U.S. President, was descended from one of these 17th-century soldiers, whilst Edinburgh's prestige in medicine was first established by 'the Monro Dynasty', three successive professors named Alexander Monro, the first born in 1697, the third dying in 1859.

**Septs:**

| | | | |
|---|---|---|---|
| DINGWALL | KIDDIE | MACKEDDIE | MUNROE |
| FOULIS | MACADIE | MACLULLICH | VASS |
| FOWLIS | MACCULLOCH | MONRO | WASS |
| KEDDIE | MACEDDIE | MONROE | |

**MURRAY**          Though a few among the Galloway Murrays may derive from 'MacMurray', most by far of this widespread clan take their name from the ancient province of Moray, which once included Inverness-shire besides the present county, and in the 12th century was the storm-centre of a series of clan rebellions against the nationally organised feudalism of Malcolm Canmore's dynasty. Under David I the 1130 revolt was suppressed and a process begun of transplanting whole clans into and out of Moray. Freskin of Strathbrock (Broxburn), said to be a Fleming, was one of the incoming leaders. He was installed at Duffus with the name de Moravia and is claimed as founder to all Clan Murray. The earliest branches were of Sutherland and Bothwell, and an important Perthshire section includes the Duke of Atholl as Chief of the Tullibardine branch. Murrays took a prominent place with Wallace and Bruce and in both Jacobite risings, as also in other spheres, such as founding the scientific Royal Society of London. The various Earls of Moray had little or no connection with the Clan Murray.

**Septs:**

| | | | |
|---|---|---|---|
| BALNEAVES | FLEMING | PIPER | SMALL |
| DINSMORE | MORAY | PYPER | SMEAL |
| DUNBAR | MURRIE | SMAIL | SPALDING |
| DUNSMORE | NEAVES | SMALE | |

**OGILVIE**          The Ogilvies descend from Gilchrist, first Earl of Angus, through his second son Gilbert, who about 1170 was granted the barony of Ogilvie near Glamis and took his name from it. Chiefship lies with the Airlie branch — 'the Bonnie Hoose' of Jacobite song. Their devotion to the Stewarts led to feuds with various neighbours like the Campbells of Dollar, and the Banffshire Ogilvies against the Gordons. The Lord Ogilvie who was exiled for his share of 'the forty-five' received command of a regiment of pre-revolutionary France that took his name.

**Septs:**

| | | | |
|---|---|---|---|
| AIRLIE | GILCHRIST | OGILVY | STORRIE |
| FINDLATER | MACGILCHRIST | RICHARDSON | |
| FUTHIE | OGILBY | STOREY | |

## ROBERTSON

Their first chief Duncan, from whom the numerous Robertsons take their alternative name Clan Donnachaidh or Donnachie, was friend and ally to King Robert Bruce and tradition had him a son of the Angus Mor mentioned under the MacDonalds. The clan remained ever active and loyal to the Stewarts and took the new name from their chief Robert (himself named after Bruce), to commemorate his capturing the murderers of James I in 1437. From the name of their ancient seat in Atholl the Chiefs retain the style Struan Robertson, but branches became distributed widely in Scotland and, indeed, throughout the world.

Septs:

| | | | |
|---|---|---|---|
| COLLIER | DONAGHY | MACDONACHIE | MACROBIE |
| COLYEAR | DUNCAN | MACGLASHAN | MACWILLIAM |
| CONNOCHIE | DUNCANSON | MACINROY | REED |
| CONOCHIE | DUNNACHIE | MACIVER | REID |
| CUNNISON | HOBSON | MACIVOR | ROBBIE |
| DOBBIE | INCHES | MACJAMES | ROBERTS |
| DOBBIN | KYNOCH | MACLAGAN | ROBISON |
| DOBIE | MACCONACHIE | MACCULLICH | ROBSON |
| DOBIESON | MACCONCHIE | MACONACHIE | ROY |
| DOBINSON | MACCONICH | MACROBBIE | STARK |
| DOBSON | MACCONECHY | MACROBERT | TONNOCHY |
| DONACHIE | MACCONNOCHIE | MACROBERTS | |

## ROSE

Around the 12th century the Norman family de Ros acquired lands in various parts of Scotland; and a small Strathnairn clan, first recorded in Alexander II's time at Geddes, early became Rose of Kilravock (pronounced 'Ross of Kilraik'). By cleverly simple diplomacy and studiously planting their own garden — as observed for instance by visitors Prince Charlie, and Cumberland the day after — the chiefs achieved respect, safety and an unbroken succession through long centuries amid contending factions. The family talent must have clung to the J. A. Rose who attained rank in the French Revolution government while saving many lives from its 'Terror', playing a role greater than his fictional counterpart 'the Scarlet Pimpernel'.

Septs:

| | | | |
|---|---|---|---|
| BARON | BARRON | GEDDES | ROSS |

## ROSS

The Norman family de Ros were established in North Ayrshire in the 12th century and from the same quarter installed a fresh branch over two centuries ago by purchasing the Balnagowan seat of the unrelated Clan Ross chiefs. Hence many Rosses in the south, in the Moray to Aberdeen sector, and some in Ross-shire itself are really of the same ancestry as Clan Rose, pronounced also Ross.

The Ross clan, otherwise Anrias from a 13th-century chief MacGilleAndreas, 'Son of a devotee of St Andrew', took name from the province of which their earliest chiefs were Earls. They served with Bruce at Bannockburn and came to possess a large section of Ross-shire but lost much power after Harlaw 1411 and the 1476 forfeiture of the earldom to the crown. In more recent times Rosses have earned front rank in such spheres as polar exploration and tropical medicine.

Septs:

| | | | |
|---|---|---|---|
| ANDERSON | DENOON | HAGGART | TAGGART |
| ANDISON | DENUNE | MACANDREW | TULLO |
| ANDREW | DINGWALL | MACCULLIE | TULLOCH |
| ANDREWS | DUTHIE | MACCULLOCH | TYRE |
| CORBET | FAIR | MACLULLICH | VASS |
| CORBETT | GAIR | MACTAGGART | WASS |
| CROW | GEAR | MACTEAR | |
| CROWE | GILLANDERS | MACTIER | |
| CROY | HAGART | MACTIRE | |

**SCOTT**     The first recorded of this surname, originally spelt Scot, was Uchtred filius Scoti ('Son of a Scot', i.e. not Saxon or Norman) about 1124, and his grandsons are believed to have founded the branches of Buccleuch and Balwearie in Fife, from which in turn came many others and a noted clan of the Border. The great Sir Walter is far from the only brilliant star among 'the Saucy Scotts'. Michael Scot, 'the Wizard' of Balwearie, contemporary scientist with the 13th-century Roger Bacon, then the 17th-century Sir John Scot of Scotstarvit, another sane eccentric, and David Scott, among our finest painters, are three that merit fuller appreciation.

**Septs:**

| | | | |
|---|---|---|---|
| GEDDES | LAIDLAW | LANGLANDS | NAPIER |

**SHAW**     The Highland Shaws were a branch of Clan Chattan and claim descent from the 12th-century Seach or Shiach mentioned as founder of the Macintosh clan. First settled at Rothiemurchus in Strathspey, with an islet-fortress in Loch nan Eilean, the clan became broken up when their Chief of 1595 was dispossessed. Sections attached themselves to Macintosh and MacPherson, whilst many migrated over the Lairig Ghru into Aberdeenshire. The playwright George Bernard Shaw descended of a Dublin branch. The name Shaw was then adopted as sounding like the original Gaelic, but in the Lowlands it means 'a small wood' and has been a family surname in Renfrewshire since the 13th century, with its own branches spreading later to Stirlingshire and through Ayrshire to Galloway.

**Septs:**

| | | |
|---|---|---|
| MACKAY | SEATH | SHEACH |
| MACHAY | SETH | SHIACH |

**SINCLAIR**     The St Clairs first arrived in England with William the Conqueror, then in the Scotland of David I a branch became settled at Roslin, near Edinburgh. From 1379 these gave name to Scotland's most northerly clan and acquired its chiefship by a marriage to the heiress of the earldom of Caithness. Apart from local feuds with the Gunns and others, Sinclairs have frequently distinguished themselves in Scottish history. One Sir William fell in Spain, 1330, with the Douglas who was bearing Bruce's heart to the Holy Land. Then to Sinclairs green is counted unlucky since so many of them wearing it fell with their Chief at Flodden, 1513. Sir John Sinclair of Ulbster, painted by Raeburn as Commander of the Fencible Regiment he raised in 1794, was a most practical idealist, forerunner of social surveys and planned agriculture and first to use the word 'statistics'.

**Septs:**

| | | |
|---|---|---|
| BUDGE | GROAT | WARES |
| CLYNE | LYALL | |

**SKENE**     The Skenes took their name from the place in Aberdeenshire they had occupied some time before Robert Bruce in 1317 granted Robert de Skene a baronial charter. W. F. Skene, the 19th-century historian of the Celts, believed his ancestor, this Robert, to be descended from an early Chief of Clan Robertson. Skene chiefs fell in several national battles, at Harlaw, Flodden and Pinkie.

**Septs:**

| | | |
|---|---|---|
| DYAS | DYCE | SKEEN |

**STEWART**     The surname Stewart is the same as Steward, indicating the offical in charge of the household and treasury, whether of the king or of some court-holding earl or bishop. It was from Walter fitz Alan, the Norman noble appointed by David I hereditary High Steward of Scotland with personal estates in Renfrewshire, that the Stewart kings descended. But Walter's influential family and descendants had established various separate branches of Stewarts before their main line attained its Royal status. This occurred through another Walter, the sixth High Steward, who fought at Bannockburn, marrying King Robert Bruce's daughter Marjory. Their son became Robert II, the first Stewart king, when David II died childless in 1371. From then on the Stewart dynasty's strengths and weaknesses, self-sacrificing leadership mingled with unremitting obstinacies, brought no little of the clan spirit into national history.

Previous to 1371, Walter's uncle, Sir John Stewart of Bonkill, who fell at Falkirk 1298, left seven sons. The first three founded respectively the Stewart earldoms of Angus, Lennox, and Galloway.

**Septs:**

| | | | |
|---|---|---|---|
| BOYD | FRANCIS | LYLE | MOODIE |
| CARMICHAEL | LENNOX | MACMICHAEL | MOODY |
| DENNISON | LISLE | MENTEITH | STEUARD |
| DENNISTON | LOMBARD | MONTEATH | STEUART |
| FRANCE | LUMBARD | MONTEITH | STUART |

## STEWART of Appin

Sir John's fourth son, Sir James Stewart of Pierston and Warwickhill, Ayrshire, who fell at Halidon Hill 1333, became ancestor to several important lines, including the Stewart Lords of Lorne and those of Atholl. The Appin clan sprang from the last Lord Lorne, who died in 1469.

**Septs:**

| | | | |
|---|---|---|---|
| CARMICHAEL | LIVINGSTON | MACDONLEAVY | MACNAIRN |
| CLAY | LIVINGSTONE | MACKINDLAY | MACNUCATOR |
| COMBE | LORNE | MACKINLAY | MACROB |
| COMBICH | MACCLAY | MACKINLEY | MACROBB |
| COMBIE | MACCLEAY | MACLAE | MITCHELL |
| CONLAY | MACCOLL | MACLAY | MITCHELSON |
| CONLEY | MACCOMBE | MACLEA | ROBB |
| DONLEVY | MACCOMBICH | MACLEAY | WALKER |
| LEAY | MACCOMBIE | MACLEW | |
| LEVACK | MACCOMIE | MACMICHAEL | |

## STEWART of Atholl

The first Stewart Earl of Atholl was Sir John of Balveny, son of Sir James Stewart, 'the Black Knight of Lorne', and Jane, widow of King James I of Scotland. But around the same time, most of the Atholl clan sprang from five sons of Sir Alexander Stewart, fourth son of Robert II, and most markedly remembered as the fierce 'Wolf of Badenoch', who died 1404.

**Septs:**

| | | | |
|---|---|---|---|
| CONACHER | CRUIKSHANK | GRAY | MACGARROW |
| CRUICKSHANK | DUILACH | LARNACH | MACGLASHAN |
| CRUICKSHANKS | GARROW | LARNACK | |

## STUART of Bute

The beautiful Isle of Bute formed part of the domain of Walter, the first High Steward, and remained a Stewart possession except for a brief Norse occupation. But only after 1385 did a family branch become established there, when Sir John Stewart, a son of King Robert II, was appointed hereditary Sheriff of Bute and Arran. His descendants still hold the marquisate of Bute.

The spelling 'Stuart' originated with some Stewarts living in France where the alphabet has no 'w'. Adopted there also by Mary Queen of Scots, it became fashionable when she continued using it on her return. Steuart was a compromise between the two forms.

**Septs:**

| | | | |
|---|---|---|---|
| BALLANTYNE | JAMIESON | MACELHERAN | MALLOY |
| BANNATYNE | LEWIS | MACKERRON | MILLOY |
| CAW | LOY | MACKIRDY | MUNN |
| FULLARTON | MACCAA | MACLEWIS | NEILSON |
| FULLERTON | MACCAMMIE | MACLOUIS | SHARP |
| GLASS | MACCAW | MACLOY | SHARPE |
| HUNTER | MACCLOY | MACMUNE | |
| JAMESON | MACCURDY | MACMURTRIE | |

## SUTHERLAND

The Clan Sutherland is an early branch from Clan Murray, as there mentioned. In 1197 Hugh, a grandson of Freskin de Moravia, was granted by William the Lion the southern portion of Caithness, named *Sudrland* while previously under Norse occupation. Hugh's son William, who died at Dunrobin Castle in 1248, was created Earl of Sutherland, which earldom remains the oldest extant in Britain.

The clan, of whom many retained the name Murray, was much embroiled in feuds with neighbours until a peace of 1591, yet figured with distinction at Bannockburn and other national battles. In the Jacobite times they took the side of government along with old rivals like the MacKays, and in contrast to their own parent clan. In 1800 they formed the 93rd or Sutherland Highlanders — the 'Thin Red Line' of Balaclava — that was joined with the Argyllshires in 1881.

**Septs:**

| | | | |
|---|---|---|---|
| CHIENE | DUFFES | GRAY | MOWATT |
| CHEYNE | DUFFUS | KEITH | MURRAY |
| CLYNE | FEDERITH | MOUAT | OLIPHANT |

## URQUHART

By tradition a very early branch from Clan Forbes, the small clan Urquhart took their name from the glen and fortress by Loch Ness that they occupied, although also settled in Cromarty as hereditary Sheriffs from at least the 14th century. Sir Thomas Urquhart of Cromarty, the celebrated translator of Rabelais, was a devoted warrior for both Charles I and Charles II and died from a fit of laughter on hearing of the latter's Restoration in 1660.

# THE SCOTTISH TARTANS

There are two main schools of thought on the origin of tartans. One view is that way back in the mists of time every Scottish family had a distinctive tartan pattern, the colours of which were obtained from the plants which grew only in their locality. The opposing view states that clans, kilts and tartan were an early 19th-century invention which the Victorians developed into an enormous cult. Somewhere between these two schools lies the truth.

What is well recorded is that the Celts were noted for their exuberant sense of colour, Roman observers referring to their striped, variegated or chequered clothing and tattoos. The simple two-colour checks of two thousand years ago have evolved through a progression of cross-checks into a profusion of differing patterns which today themselves number well over two thousand. 'Tartan' itself is a word originally imported from Europe, the Gaels using the term *breacan*, meaning 'speckled' or 'multicoloured'. The word 'plaid' is from the Gaelic word for blanket, being either a bedcover or a length of cloth perhaps 12 feet by 5 feet which was swathed around the wearer and belted at the waist, hence the term 'belted plaid'. The essentially white-based, patterned household blankets which went with the early Scots settlers to North America evoked an admiration for the pretty 'plaid patterns', and in time 'plaid' itself became a synonym for tartan and of arguably older origin.

Gaelic poetry and recorded observations, back to at least the 16th century, associate certain setts of tartan with specific families, but no more than a handful. However, tartan was of sufficient importance by the time of the 1745 Rising that its aftermath saw a severely shaken government rush through an Act of Parliament in 1746 which banned the wearing of 'tartan, kilt and plaid' by all civilian men and boys other than landowners. That Act was not repealed until 1782, and in the ensuing period of restoration for Scotland's shattered pride a series of cultural traditions were revived or invented which served to confuse the historical realities concerning what was to become the national dress for all Scotland.

Tartans and Highland dress were not regimented until the Scottish regiments themselves adopted standard-pattern uniforms, and quaint Victorian customs such as the wearing of 'dress' tartans after 6 p.m. do not detract from the venerable pedigree of non-military Highland dress, stretching back at least three hundred years.

It is an old Highland tradition to encourage guests to wear our unique mode of dress. We should regard it as a compliment. For the wearer who has no tartan associated with his surname, there are certain options available:

1. Wear that which is connected to your maternal or any other of your family lines.
2. Wear the sett appropriate to the district from which your family comes or in which your surname was known.
3. Wear the Jacobite or Caledonian setts, or even the Government or 'Black Watch' pattern if you are not pro-Stuart.
4. Wear whichever you prefer, but remember that when you sport a tartan you are proclaiming allegiance to that chief and his clan. Your loyalties may be tested!

| | |
|---|---|
| ABERDEEN | BUCHANAN |
| ANDERSON | CAMERON |
| ANGUS | CAMERON of Erracht |
| ARMSTRONG | CAMERON of Lochiel |
| ATHOLL DISTRICT | CAMPBELL of Argyll |
| AUSTIN (and KEITH) | Dress CAMPBELL of Argyll |
| BAIRD | CAMPBELL of Breadalbane |
| BALMORAL | CAMPBELL of Cawdor |
| BARCLAY | CAMPBELL of Loudoun |
| Dress BARCLAY | CARNEGIE |
| BLACK WATCH (42nd Regimental) | CHISHOLM |
| BLAIR LOGIE | Hunting CHISHOLM |
| BRODIE | CLERGY |
| Hunting BRODIE | COCKBURN |
| BRUCE | COLQUHOUN |

CRANSTON
CRAWFORD
CRIEFF
CUMMING
Hunting CUMMING
CUNNINGHAM
DALZIEL
DAVIDSON
DAVIDSON of Tulloch
DOUGLAS
DOUGLAS (Grey)
DRUMMOND (Same as GRANT)
Old DRUMMOND
DRUMMOND of Strathallan
DUNBAR
DUNBLANE
DUNCAN
DUNDAS
DUNDEE
DYCE
EDINBURGH
ELLIOT
ERSKINE
FARQUHARSON
FERGUSON
FERGUSON of Balquhidder
FLETCHER
FLETCHER of Dunans
FORBES
FORT WILLIAM
FORTY-SECOND (BLACK WATCH)
Dress FORTY-SECOND
FRASER
Hunting FRASER
GALLOWAY DISTRICT
Dress GALLOWAY (Red)
Hunting GALLOWAY (Green)
GLASGOW
GLEN LYON DISTRICT
GLEN ORCHY DISTRICT
GORDON
Dress GORDON
Old GORDON
GOW and MACGOWAN
GRAHAM of Monteith
GRAHAM of Montrose
GRANT
GRANT of Glenmoriston
GUNN
Old GUNN
HAMILTON
HAY
HENDERSON and MACKENDRICK
HOME
HOPE-VERE
HUNTLY DISTRICT

INNES
JACOBITE
JOHNSTON
KEITH and AUSTIN
KENNEDY
KERR
LAMONT
LAUDER
LEITH-HAY
LENNOX
LESLIE
Dress LESLIE (Red)
LINDSAY
LIVINGSTONE
LOGAN or MACLENNAN
MACALISTER
MACALPINE
MACARTHUR
MACAULAY
Hunting MACAULAY
MACBEAN
MACBETH
MACCALLUM
Old MACCALLUM
MACDIARMID
MACDONALD of the Isles
Dress MACDONALD of the Isles
Old MACDONALD of the Isles
MACDONALD of Sleat
Dress MACDONALD of Sleat
Old MACDONALD of Sleat
MACDONALD (or MACIAN) of
    Ardnamurchan
MACDONALD of Clanranald
Hunting MACDONALD of Clanranald
MACDONALD of Kingsburgh
MACDONALD of Staffa (or Boisdale)
MACDONNELL of Glengarry
Hunting MACDONNELL of Glengarry
MACDONNELL of Keppoch
MACDOUGALL
MACDUFF
Hunting MACDUFF
MACEWAN
MACFARLANE
MACFARLANE (Black and White)
MACFIE
MACGILLIVRAY
MACGOWAN or GOW
MACGREGOR
MACGREGOR Rob Roy
MACHARDY
MACIAN (See MACDONALD)
MACINNES
Hunting MACINNES
MACINROY

MACINTOSH
MACINTYRE
Dress MACINTYRE (Red)
MACINTYRE of Glenorchy
MACIVOR
MACKAY
MACKENDRICK or HENDERSON
MACKENZIE
MACKINLAY
MACKINNON
Hunting MACKINNON
MACLACHLAN
Dress MACLACHLAN
Old MACLACHLAN
MACLAINE of Lochbuie
Hunting MACLAINE of Lochbuie
MACLAREN
MACLEAN of Duart
Hunting MACLEAN of Duart
MACLENNAN or LOGAN
MACLEOD of Harris (and of Skye)
MACLEOD of Harris (Black and white)
MACLEOD of Harris (Black and red)
MACLEOD of Lewis (and of Raasay and
   Assynt)
Dress MACLEOD of Lewis
MACMILLAN
Hunting MACMILLAN
MACNAB
MACNAUGHTON
MACNEIL of Barra
MACNEILL of Gigha (and of Colonsay)
MACNICOL or NICOLSON
MACPHERSON
Old 'Hunting' MACPHERSON (Grey
   ground)
Dress MACPHERSON (White)
MACQUARRIE
MACQUEEN
MACRAE (Green)
Dress MACRAE (Red)
Hunting MACRAE
MACRAE of Conchra
MACTAGGART
MACTAVISH
MACTHOMAS (Ancient and Modern)
MALCOLM
MATHESON
Hunting MATHESON
MAXWELL
MELVILLE
MENZIES (Red and white)
MENZIES (Black and red)
MENZIES (Black and white)
Hunting MENZIES
MIDDLETON

MONTGOMERY
Old MONTGOMERY
MORRISON
MOUAT
MULL DISTRICT
MUNRO
Dress MUNRO (Red)
MURRAY of Atholl
MURRAY of Tullibardine
NAPIER
NICOLSON or MACNICOL
OGILVIE
Hunting OGILVIE (Green)
OLIPHANT
PAISLEY
RAMSAY
RATTRAY
ROB ROY (MacGregor)
ROBERTSON
Hunting ROBERTSON
ROSE
Dress ROSE (Red)
ROSS
Hunting ROSS
ROXBURGH DISTRICT
RUSSELL
RUTHVEN
SCOTT
Hunting SCOTT
SCOTT (Black and white)
SINCLAIR
Hunting SINCLAIR
SKENE
SKENE (Yellow stripe)
Royal STEWART (Red)
Royal STEWART (White, Prince
   Charles Edward)
Dress STEWART
Hunting STEWART
STEWART (Black ground)
STEWART (Black and white)
STEWART of Appin
Old STEWART of Appin
STEWART of Atholl
STEWART of Galloway
STUART of Bute
STRATHEARN
SUTHERLAND
Old SUTHERLAND
TWEEDSIDE DISTRICT
URQUHART
Old URQUHART
WALLACE
Old WALLACE
WEMYSS
Old WEMYSS

# A GLOSSARY OF TERMS

**THE LION RAMPANT**   The Scottish Lion, as worn on Royal and princely shields.

**THE HARP OF THE HEBRIDES**   In early times the harp was the principal musical instrument.

**HIGHLAND CATTLE**   These strong, shaggy animals are natives of the Highlands and are to be seen grazing on the hillsides and plains, looking as picturesque as their rugged surroundings.

**JOHN KNOX AT HOLYROOD PALACE**   When Mary Queen of Scots returned from France in 1561, after thirteen years' absence, she tried to re-establish the Roman Catholic Religion. John Knox, a native of Haddington, and an outstanding figure during the Reformation, preached in St Giles Cathedral against her practices. She summoned him to Holyrood and used every argument against him, but she soon found that he was to be her most bitter enemy during her reign and that the Reformed Church was firmly established.

**HOLYROOD ABBEY**   The Abbey was built by King David I in 1128. The ruined Church still remains. Here took place the marriages of James II, James III, and James IV, and that of Queen Mary and Lord Darnley. It contains the graves of kings and queens of Scotland, and many other distinguished persons. In 1429, James I received, from the High Altar, the submission of Alexander, Lord of the Isles.

**MARY QUEEN OF SCOTS AT HOLYROOD PALACE**   A halo of romance surrounds Mary Queen of Scots and Holyrood. Her life there was one of splendour and gaiety. She was one of the most beautiful women of her time. By her fearless courage and winsome manners, she made many friends, but her impulsiveness and indiscretion often brought trouble upon her and endangered the lives of others. Her lover, Rizzio, was murdered in the Palace, and from here she fled with Bothwell after the unfortunate death of her husband, Darnley.

**THE LORD OF THE ISLES AND HIS CHIEFS**   The MacDonalds, Lords of the Isles and Earls of Ross, descended from Somerled, son of Gilliebride, of the 11th century. They represented a race of famous warriors, their influence and power being so great at one period as to threaten the Scottish king. The clans of the Western Isles and the greater part of the Highlands were under their domination until the 13th century.

**THE PIPERS**   The MacCruimins were the most celebrated pipers in the Highlands. They were Hereditary Pipers to the MacLeods. 'Oil-Thigh', a college, was kept by them for the instruction of pipe music. They have many compositions to their illustrious name.

**SAINT COLUMBA**   Saint Columba arrived on our shores, on the island of Iona, in 563. He set up the first Celtic Church there and prepared his twelve apostles for the spreading of the Christian religion. He was connected with the Royal House of Leinster and the Kings of Dalriada.

**HOLYROOD PALACE**   The Palace was founded by James IV, in 1501, and was the residence of the Scottish Kings. It has witnessed many splendid gatherings. The Picture Gallery, the largest apartment of the Palace, was the scene of much splendour when 'Bonnie Prince Charlie' held his levées and balls there in 1745.

**PRINCE CHARLES BIDS FAREWELL TO FLORA MACDONALD**
Through the calmness, courage and devotion of a young lady, Flora MacDonald, Prince Charles made good his miraculous escape, from Benbecula to Skye, from the very presence of his pursuers. Dressed as her Irish serving maid, he was conducted by her to friends who conveyed him to a more secure hiding-place on the mainland until his escape to France could be made possible.

**MARY QUEEN OF SCOTS IN LOCH LEVEN CASTLE**   After the death of Darnley, her husband, Queen Mary was imprisoned in Loch Leven Castle. She was made to sign a document whereby she abdicated the Scottish throne in favour of her son, James. On the death of Elizabeth, Queen of England, James ascended the English throne, thus uniting the two crowns.

**MARY QUEEN OF SCOTS ESCAPES FROM LOCH LEVEN CASTLE**   A page named William Douglas got possession of the keys of the Castle. He hurried to the Queen and bade her proceed to the outer gate while he locked the doors, thus preventing immediate pursuit. As they rowed to the mainland, Douglas threw the keys into the loch.

**JAMES V VISITS THE CLANS**   In 1540 James V sailed to the Western Isles with twelve well-appointed ships carrying troops and artillery. The cabins were hung with silk and carried pavilions for erection wherever the King might choose to land. He made friends with many of the clan chiefs and invited them to join the Royal party, but afterwards betrayed them.

**PRINCE CHARLES AND HIS FRIENDS**   After the Battle of Culloden, Prince Charles made his way to the west coast. He went from place to place, and clan to clan, guarded and concealed by loyal Highlanders, while 500 regulars and militia combed the countryside for his capture. There was a reward of £30,000 on his head.

**JAMES V MEETS THE CHIEFS**   With pomp and splendour King James V visited the chiefs. He persuaded many of them to join the Royal tour, professing to be on the most friendly terms. When the ships reached Dumbarton, the King landed, but the chiefs, unsuspecting of the treachery of the King, were taken to Edinburgh, where they were imprisoned. Some remained there until the King's death.

**RAISING THE STANDARD AT GLENFINNAN**   On 23rd July 1745, Prince Charles Edward, grandson of the exiled King James, arrived on our shores to stir up the Jacobite cause. At the head of Loch Shiel, in the Valley of Glenfinnan, on 19th August, the Standard was raised by the aged Tullibardine, Duke of Atholl.

**HIGHLAND DANCING**   Highland Gatherings are held at different periods of the year at Oban, Dunoon, Luss, Braemar, Inverness, Aberdeen, etc. The day's programme includes Highland dancing, pipe music, sports and games. The March-past of the Pipers and the Highland Fling are favourite items.

**THE FIERY CROSS**   A cross made of wood, charred at one end, with a piece of white linen, dipped in goat's blood, hanging from the other represented the Fiery Cross, which was used as a symbol of war to call out the clans. Failure by a chief to obey its summons was punishable by death.

**THE MASSACRE OF GLENCOE**   In 1692 the MacDonalds of Glencoe were brutally attacked and massacred by the Campbells, who were given a signed order to extirpate the clan. One hundred and twenty of the MacDonalds, including the chief's two sons, escaped through the deep snow to the hills and glens.

**THE BATTLE OF LARGS**   The Norwegian army was defeated by Alexander III at the Battle of Largs in 1263, as a result of which Norway surrendered the Hebrides to Scotland on the payment of 4,000 marks and an agreed annual payment of 100 marks.

**A NORSEMAN RAID**   These Vikings were a menace to Scotland in early times. They invaded her shores, plundered and burned the homes of the people, and carried off men, women and children as slaves.

**CLAN BATTLE OF THE SUTHERLANDS**   Many clan battles were fought between legitimate heirs to titles and illegitimate sons. Such was the case in the 16th century in the history of the Sutherlands. The unfortunate son's head, after the battle, was hoisted on a spear on the tower of Dunrobin Castle. He had boasted that the witches had foretold 'that his head should be the highest that ever was of the Sutherlands'.

**INVERNESS CASTLE**   The present Castle stands on the site of the ancient residence of the early Pictish Kings, this being the capital of the kingdom.

**COLUMBA MEETS BRUDE**   Two years after Saint Columba arrived at Iona, he visited Brude, King of the Northern Picts, who readily became a convert to the new religion. The tribes followed the example of their King, and soon Columba's doctrine spread throughout Scotland.

**WALLACE'S MONUMENT**   This monument was erected in 1869 to mark the defeat of the English in 1297 at the Battle of Stirling Bridge by William Wallace, a great Scottish hero. He was a native of Elderslie, near Paisley. The tower, which is 200 feet high, commands a magnificent view of the 'Windings of the River Forth', with its fertile valleys and amphitheatre of hills.

**BRUCE AND DE BOHUN**   To the standard of Robert the Bruce, Scotland's most valorous king, the Highland clans and Scottish lowland families rallied in one great effort to free their country from the yoke of the English king. The evening before the memorable victory of Bannockburn, an English knight, Sir Henry De Bohun, rode against the Scottish king, thinking to make him an easy prey. Bruce raised himself on his steed, swung its head aside, and with one blow of his battle-axe brought the ambitious knight to the ground.

**DRUM CLOG**   In 1679, near Loudon Hill, a body of Covenanters fought, and gained a victory over, Claverhouse and his troops.

**A BORDER RAID**   The Scots and the English had many wars over the northern counties of England, and the Lothians of Scotland. As a result, the Border countries were always in a state of turmoil and destruction. This state existed until the Union of the Crowns in 1603.

**CULLODEN**   The Jacobite army was completely routed by Cumberland and the Royal forces at Culloden Moor in 1746. Prince Charles with some of his chiefs and clansmen escaped to the hills and glens, whilst the troops were given orders to search for them and put them to the sword. In this way many met their death. The wounded and dying were massacred on the battlefield.

**THE MARCH FROM GLENFINNAN**   From Glenfinnan Charles and the Highland army marched towards Edinburgh. At Perth they were received with great rejoicing. The people subscribed liberally to their funds, and many from the clans in the district joined their ranks.

**STIRLING CASTLE**   For centuries, Stirling Castle was the favourite residence of Scottish kings. It was the birthplace of James II, James III, and James IV. James VI spent the first thirteen years of his life here. It is one of Scotland's most ancient and historical fortresses.

**CROWNING OF THE SCOTTISH KINGS**   The MacDuffs had the honour of crowning the Scottish kings. In 838 the Coronation Stone was brought to Scone and remained there until King Edward I removed it to England in 1296.

**EDINBURGH CASTLE**   Edinburgh Castle was impregnable as an ancient stronghold. It is now an infantry barracks. Because of its history and associations, it forms a subject of great interest to all visitors to the capital. In the Throne Room the Regalia of Scotland is kept.

**BRUCE AND THE RED COMYN**   Robert the Bruce and Sir John Comyn claimed the right to the Scottish throne. They met in a church in Dumfries when, during an argument, Bruce drew his dagger and wounded Comyn. He rushed outside and told his friends, Kirkpatrick and Lindsay, what he had done. 'I'll mak' sikkar', said Kirkpatrick, who then entered the church and killed the wounded man.

**A SCOTTISH DESIGN**
1. The Saint Andrew's Cross or Scottish National Ensign.
2. The Thistle or Scottish National Emblem.
3. Heather and the Scottish blue bell.

**THE MONARCH OF THE GLEN**   There are many deer forests in the Highlands. The deer is commonly called 'The Monarch of the Glen'.

**ROYAL DEESIDE**   The Highland Royal residence, Balmoral Castle, is situated close by the River Dee. The estate is extensive, covering about 25,000 acres, much of which is deer forest.

**THE BATTLE OF HARLAW**   The title of the Earldom of Ross was contested by Donald, Lord of the Isles, on behalf of his wife. In 1411, he marched to Harlaw with 10,000 men, against an army sent by the Regent, Albany, on behalf of his son, under the command of the Earl of Mar. The two armies withdrew, completely exhausted, so that the battle was neither lost nor won. Albany, later, forced Donald to sign a treaty surrendering all claims to the title.

**A LOWLAND LANDSCAPE**   The beauty of the Lowlands cannot be exaggerated. Although not so mountainous and rugged as the Highlands, the countryside possesses a charm which arrests the attention of travellers and has inspired the pens of authors and poets.

**A BORDER RAID**   The people of the Borders suffered much from invasion. In this case it would appear that the English had been the victors, but the position was often the reverse, when the Scots would be in possession of the plunder.

**VIKINGS**   The Vikings were sea pirates who, in early history, landed and plundered wherever they chose.

**PRINCESS MARGARET ARRIVES FROM NORWAY**   The Princess Margaret married James III of Scotland. Her father, King Christian of Norway, Sweden and Denmark, gave as her dowry the Orkney and Shetland Islands. He also cancelled the debt that had been owing since the reign of James I. This debt was the result of an agreement after the Battle of Largs.

**THE BATTLE OF FLODDEN**   There was scarcely a home that did not mourn the loss of a father, son or relative after this battle which was a sad disaster in the history of Scotland. It was fought in 1513, and the Scottish King James IV and many of his nobles were slain.

# List of Battles

| | |
|---|---|
| Aberdeen | 13 September 1644 |
| Alford | 2 July 1645 |
| Ancrum Moor | 27 February 1545 |
| Annan | 25 December 1332 |
| Auldearn | 9 May 1645 |
| Bannockburn | 24 June 1314 |
| Bothwell Bridge | 22 June 1679 |
| Bridge of Dee | 19 June 1639 |
| Carbisdale | 27 April 1650 |
| Cromdale | 1 May 1690 |
| Culloden | 16 April 1746 |
| Dalnaspidal | 26 July 1654 |
| Drumclog | 1 June 1679 |
| Dunbar | 3 September 1650 |
| Dundee | 4 April 1645 |
| Dunkeld | 21 August 1689 |
| Dunnichen | 20 May 1685 |
| Dunsinane | 27 July 1054 |
| Dupplin Moor | 12 August 1332 |
| Falkirk I | 22 July 1298 |
| Falkirk II | 17 January 1746 |
| Flodden | 9 September 1513 |
| Fyvie | 28 October 1644 |
| Glenlivet | 3 October 1594 |
| Glenshiel | 10 June 1719 |
| Halidon Hill | 19 July 1333 |
| Harlaw | 24 July 1411 |
| Inverlochy | 2 February 1645 |
| Killicrankie | 27 July 1689 |
| Kilsyth | 15 August 1645 |
| Langside | 13 May 1568 |
| Largs | 2 October 1263 |
| Lochmaben | 22 July 1484 |
| Lumphanan | 15 August 1057 |
| Meldrum | 22 May 1308 |
| Methven | 19 June 1306 |
| Otterburn | 19 August 1388 |
| Philiphaugh | 13 September 1645 |
| Pinkie | 10 September 1547 |
| Prestonpans | 21 September 1745 |
| Renfrew | 20 October 1164 |
| Sark | 23 October 1448 |
| Sauchieburn | 11 June 1488 |
| Sheriffmuir | 13 November 1715 |
| Solway Moss | 24 November 1542 |
| Stirling Bridge | 11 September 1297 |
| Tippermuir | 1 September 1644 |

# List of Scottish Sovereigns

| | | | |
|---|---|---|---|
| Malcolm II | 1005-1034 | First Interregnum | 1290-1292 |
| Duncan I | 1034-1040 | John Baliol | 1292-1296 |
| Macbeth | 1040-1057 | Second Interregnum | 1296-1306 |
| Malcolm III (Canmore) | 1057-1093 | Robert I | 1306-1329 |
| Donald Bane | 1093-1094 | David II | 1329-1371 |
| Duncan II | 1094-1094 | Robert II | 1371-1390 |
| Donald Bane (2nd Reign) | 1094-1097 | Robert III | 1390-1406 |
| Edgar | 1097-1107 | James I | 1406-1437 |
| Alexander I | 1107-1124 | James II | 1437-1460 |
| David I | 1124-1153 | James III | 1460-1488 |
| Malcolm IV | 1153-1165 | James IV | 1488-1513 |
| William (The Lion) | 1165-1214 | James V | 1513-1542 |
| Alexander II | 1214-1249 | Mary | 1542-1567 |
| Alexander III | 1249-1286 | James VI | 1567-1625 |
| Margaret (Maid of Norway) | 1286-1290 | | |

# Some Sources of Further Information

*Organisations*
The Council of Scottish Clan Associations, P.O. Box 27268, Houston, Texas 77227
The Scottish International Gathering Trust, 25 Dublin Street, Edinburgh EH1 3PB
  (0131-557 4059)
The Scottish Tartans Society, Davidson House, Drummond Street, Comrie, Perthshire
The Scots Ancestry Research Society, 3 Albany Street, Edinburgh EH1 3PY (0131-556 4220)


*Books*
Adam, Frank *The Clans, Septs and Regiments of the Scottish Highlands* Edinburgh 1970
Black, George F. *The Surnames of Scotland: Their Origin, Meaning and History*
  New York 1946
Dorward, David *Scottish Surnames* Edinburgh 1985: *Scotland's Place Names* Edinburgh
  1983
Hanks, Patrick and Hodges, Flavia *A Dictionary of Surnames* Oxford 1988
*Old Scots Surnames* Dalkeith 1982
*World Directory of Scottish Societies* Edinburgh 1980